Unleash Greatness in Your Child

Powerful,

Character–Building,

Positive

Parenting Activities

An "I Care" Positive Parenting Workbook

No part of this "I Care" *Unleash the Greatness in Your Child* Workbook may be reproduced in whole or in part, or stored in a retrieval system, or transmitted in any form or by any means electronic, mechanical, photocopied, recorded, or otherwise without express written permission of the publisher, "I Care" Products & Services.

Schools and school systems **do not** have permission to copy any part of this book for use as instructional material. Each Workbook is intended for individual use.

All of the logos, artwork, designs, and activities in this Workbook are exclusively owned by "I Care" Products & Services and are protected under copyright law.

Written by Elbert D. Solomon, Thelma S. Solomon, and Martha Ray Dean
Book design and illustrations by Phillip L. Harper, Jr.

ISBN: 1–891187–05–8
3rd Grade; First Edition
Copyright© May, 2006 by "I Care" Products & Services
E–mail: parents6@icarenow.com
www.icarenow.com/parents.html
All rights reserved. Printed in the U.S.A.

Table of Contents

Introduction

The "Unleash the Greatness in Your Child" Workbook

The "Unleash the Greatness in Your Child" Workbook will not only increase the impact that you can have on the social, emotional, and academic growth of your children, but it can help them to reach their fullest potential. Highly successful individuals share a number of traits in common. Among them are the thinking skills, attitudes, and behavior patterns that represent "character." This book provides tools for parents like you who want to begin unleashing the potential in their children through the development of their character.

Positive Parenting

Positive parenting strengthens parent/child relationships by engaging children with the most important teachers they will ever have—their parents. Furthermore, it increases academic achievement and expectations for the future; instills self–esteem and confidence; and reduces behavior problems and school absenteeism.

Character Development

Character development doesn't just happen, it is primarily learned from role models and significant adults and should be started at an early age. A list of the twelve "Pillars of Character" upon which the "I Care" approach is based is found on pages iv and v, along with the behaviors that define them at each grade level of the "I Care" Positive Parenting Workbooks.

"I Care"

Beginning over ten years ago, "I Care" is committed to communicating with parents the importance of their involvement with their children and helping them improve their parenting skills. Today, "I Care" is used by over a million parents.

"I Care" Positive Parenting & Mentoring Curricula

"I Care" Positive Parenting & Mentoring Curricula are used in over 35,000 classrooms for Toddler and Pre–K through High School. Activities similar to the ones in this Workbook are implemented by parents throughout the school year. Administrators, teachers, and parents have all raved about the results.

Feedback

Feedback is one of the key components to the "I Care" approach. Defining parental involvement as the number of positive interactions you have with your child makes it easy. The *Reflection Activity* at the end of each month will help you keep track of your involvement. The other indicator will be the changes you see in your child. They will be stunning.

Copyright© 2006 "I Care" Products & Services   (3rd Grade)

How To Use This Book

Practice, Practice, Practice

Practice is necessary for a behavior or attitude to become a habit. That's why we provide so many activities for each character trait. In fact, learning theory tells us that it generally takes 21 days of practice before a new habit is acquired. But don't stop with ours! Be creative in developing your own activities as well.

Discuss, Discuss, Discuss

Discuss—not tell, tell, tell—is the rule. If a child can talk about an idea using his own words, ask questions about it, and consider it from different points of view, he will both learn it and understand it more completely.

Parenting Activities

Carefully read through the month's activities. Designate a visible location to place the positive message and post the activities (refrigerator, message board, etc.). The activities can be done while walking or riding in the car, at the breakfast table, at bedtime, on weekends, and in other situations where you and your child are together. Take advantage of the "teachable moments" and read to and with your child daily.

Monthly Character Traits

There are twelve important character traits, one for each month of the year, spiraling from a Pillar of Character. They instill self–esteem, positive attitudes, and self–confidence. Focus on one character trait per month and complete the associated parenting, enrichment, reinforcement, positive message (monthly character trait), and reflection activities.

Parenting Pledge

The *Parenting Pledge* is an affirmation from the parent to the child that the character traits will be practiced and reinforced. Display it in a visible location. (See page vii.)

Child's Pledge

The *Child's Pledge* is an affirmation from the child to the parents. Have your child repeat it often until it is committed to memory. Display it in your child's room. (See page ix.)

Enrichment Activities

The *Enrichment Activities* will get your child excited and motivated about learning. The activities are designed to enhance your child's skills in reading, writing, constructing, designing, recognizing, visualizing, making patterns, and communicating.

Positive Messages

The monthly *Positive Message* should be displayed in a visible location to help your

child maintain focus on one character trait while you, as a parent, provide reinforcement actions.

Reinforcement Activities

These *Reinforcement Activities* will give parent and child multiple opportunities to manipulate and model the behaviors associated with each character trait during the month.

Reading Activities

The recommended books and reading activities support the child's literacy development and reinforce the monthly character traits. These books may be available at your local library or they can be purchased in a set of 12 at www.icarenow.com/parents.html. Other books that reinforce the month's concept may be used if the recommended books are unavailable.

Reflection Activity

The monthly *Reflection Activity* is designed for parents to summarize their positive actions, recognize their accomplishments, and encourage self–initiation of more positive parent/child interactions.

Successful Parenting Practices

The timeless successful parenting practices at the end of each month's activities were used as a guide to develop the "I Care" Positive Parenting Workbook. They serve as models for effective parent/child relationships.

12 Universal Pillars of Character

Goal Setting—*Learning How to Plan*

Self–Aware—*Understanding What You Think and Why*

Value Achievement—*Taking Pride in Accomplishments*

Value Others—*Being Able to See the Good in Everyone*

Self–Control—*Keeping Action and Emotion in Check*

Caring—*Respecting Others' Feelings and Giving of One's Self*

Responsible—*Following Through on Commitments*

Citizenship—*Showing Loyalty to the Rights of Others*

Life–Long Learner—*Enhancing Learning Skills*

Self–Confidence—*Trusting in Your Own Abilities*

Respect—*Showing Honor or Esteem*

Trustworthiness—*Being Honest*

"I Care" Positive Parenting Workbooks

- Built on twelve universally recognized pillars of good character with spiraling grade–level character traits to build one behavior on another
- Includes the primary behaviors that define each character trait for the repetition that enables transfer of learning
- Includes parenting/mentoring, enrichment, reinforcement, visual learning, and reflection activities
- Additional grade–level workbooks are available for the grades listed below

Month	Pillars of Charac-ter	Pre–K	Kinder-garten	1st Grade	2nd Grade	3rd Grade	4th Grade	5th Grade	6th Grade
January	Goal–Setting	Dream	Dream	Imagine	Hard Work	Persevere	Persist	Set Goals	Plan
February	Self–Aware	Recognize Feelings	Recognize Feelings	Sensitive	Humility	Consis-tency	Monitor Thinking	Integrity	Set Per-sonal Standards
March	Value Achieve-ment	Recognize Achieve-ment	Recognize Achieve-ment	Accom-plish-ments	Accept Recogni-tion	Dedication	Apprecia-tion	Productive Thinking	Push Lim-its of Abilities
April	Value Others	Unique Qualities	Unique Qualities	Make Friends	Value Dif-ferences	Hospitable	Forgive-ness	Loyalty	Tolerance
May	Self–Control	Self–Control	Self–Control	Self–Discipline	Cautious	Punctual	Endur-ance	Control Impulses	Respond to Feed-back
June	Caring	Caring	Caring	Respect	Compas-sion	Gentle	Generous	Sympa-thetic	Depend-ability
July	Responsi-ble	Responsi-ble	Responsi-ble	Follow Proce-dures	Depend-able	Prudence	Thorough	Accuracy	Willing to Accept Blame
August	Citizen-ship	Positive Attitude Toward School	Positive Attitude Toward School	School Pride	Oversee Environ-ment	Under-stand Con-sequences	Thrifti-ness	Coopera-tion	Stands for Right
September	Life–Long Learner	Read	Read	Discover	Listen	Alertness	Creative	Find Facts	Express Feelings
October	Self–Confi-dence	Self–Confi-dence	Self–Confi-dence	Self–Reliance	Optimism	Courage	Joyful	Problem Solving	Right Choices
November	Respect	Courteous	Courteous	Polite	Fairness	Patience	Honor	Open–Minded	Positive Attitude
December	Trustwor-thy	Honest	Honest	Sincere	Loyalty	Truthful	Reliable	Self–Knowl-edge	Virtuous

A Proven Educational Method

"I Care" follows best strategies of the teaching and learning process described below and has been professionally developed using relevant research.

Advanced Organizers

The *Message to Parents* is provided for introducing the month's character trait.

Three Essential Learning Conditions

These have been identified by cognitive psychologists and embedded into the workbook: reception, availability, and activation.

1. Reception—Advanced organizers focus the child's attention on specific activities.
2. Availability—Parents can take advantage of the "teachable moments" and insert parenting activities into the home schedule at any time.
3. Activation—When parents role model the character traits and ask questions such as those provided in the preplanned activities, they are activating the child's cognitive assimilation of the trait.

Repetition, Repetition, Repetition

Long–term memory is enhanced by the number of times a child mentally manipulates a trait. "I Care" provides varied repetitions of each character trait over an extended period of time. Learning theory tells us that it generally takes 21 days of practice before a new habit is acquired.

Use of Questioning Strategies

Most of the "I Care" Activities are written in the form of open–ended questions.

Connected to Real Life

Children are able to respond to activity questions (passive activity) utilizing their own experiences, and when activities involve doing something (active activity), children carry out the activity within a familiar environment that is part of their daily lives.

Substantive Conversation

Research shows that a child must talk about an idea or trait using his or her own words, ask questions about it, and look at it from multiple points of view for it to be assimilated to the point that the trait transfers into automatic behavior response. The "I Care" Workbook has built–in opportunities for all these kinds of conversations.

Parenting Activities

Message to Parents

Children who are just learning the extent of their capabilities need encouragement not to give up when the going gets rough. The sense of accomplishment they get from doing something difficult is important for building self–esteem and motivating them in the future.

1. COMMUNICATION

If at First You Don't Succeed . . .

Share some of the things you have achieved with perseverance. What special skills or degrees do you have? Do you have hobbies or play a sport where you developed your talents with hard work and practice? Talk about what these achievements have meant to you. Point out that the work was often tedious and frustrating but that by persevering, you developed your talent and skills, created some wonderful things, and accomplished much.

2. ROLE PLAYING

Model It

"I don't give up!"—Make that your motto and teach it to your child. A "can do" attitude will be catching.

Persevere

Parenting Activities

3. TABLE TALK

Talk About It

Discuss the following with your child:
- How do parents have to persevere with their children?
- In what ways do friends sometimes need to practice perseverance?
- "If at first you don't succeed, try, try again." What does that mean?
- What are some of the things that take perseverance for you to do?
- Let's memorize these sayings: "I don't procrastinate."; "It's kind of fun to do the impossible."

4. WRITING

The Power of Perseverance

Did you know that Thomas Edison tried over 10,000 experiments before he got his idea for a light bulb to work? He never thought of giving up, and when someone asked him how he kept going, he told them he hadn't failed, he was learning all the ways it wouldn't work. Get a biography of Thomas Edison from the library and read it with your child. Then, have him write a story about someone who had to persevere to overcome an obstacle, whether it was a physical handicap, like Christopher Reeve; people telling you your idea wouldn't work, like the Wright brothers; or a child who is new to the neighborhood and doesn't know anyone.

　　　　Copyright© 2006 "I Care" Products & Services   (3rd Grade)

Persevere

Parenting Activities

5. PHYSICAL

Give It a Try

Nothing encourages children to persevere more than achievement. Help your child develop a new skill. How about handling money, sewing on a button, making a cake, shoveling snow, or raking leaves? These are all activities where the results tell you how well you've done.

6. READING

Believe It

Uncle Jed's Barbershop by Margaree King Mitchell is a tender story about how Uncle Jed must have felt with each setback, and what kept him believing that he would see his dream come true.

Persevere

Parenting Activities

7. COMMUNITY

Farming

Imagine having to be on the job in 100° weather, three feet of snow, or in the pouring rain at 5:00 in the morning. That's what it takes to be a farmer. Learn more about the perseverance required by these hard–working citizens. Visit a farm in person, online, or in a book. What keeps these men and women motivated to work as hard as they do? To get just a little idea of what their life is like, get up at 4:30 a.m. every day for a week. How does it feel?

Positive Parenting Practices

- Where's the line between encouraging perseverance and being a pushy parent? It's hard to know. If your child has made a commitment to a team and the other team members are counting on him for the season, "I don't like it" is not a good enough reason. If he is just learning a new sport, instrument, or skill, he needs to keep at it to get "over the hump." But, in all cases, stay alert to what is happening with him, be encouraging, and keep talking. If you decide "enough is enough," it will be based on the facts as well as his feelings.

Persevere

Enrichment Activity

Activity 1: Art-Mouth Painting

Have you ever heard of Joni Eareckson Tada, Averill Scott Barkhouse, or Itzhak Adir? They are all mouth painters—people who have become well known artists despite the fact that they can't hold a paintbrush, except with their mouth. There are equally talented foot painters. Go online or to the public library to find examples of their work. Talk with your child about the perseverance it must have taken these artists to perfect their talent. Then, each of you can try mouth painting for yourselves, following the directions below.

Pull up a chair to the refrigerator door, then tape a piece of paper to it at face level if you were sitting in a chair. (Using the refrigerator as an easel will make it easy to clean up any lines that slip off the paper. But if you have a different area, such as a garage, that you prefer to use, please feel free to do so, but keep in mind that this project can get messy.) Use long markers to begin with, holding them in your teeth. Outline a simple shape, like a cat or a dog. Add some details and fill the shape in with some color. What are the results? Try again. Are the results any better this time? Imagine the perseverance it takes to become really good.

Persevere

Enrichment Activity

Activity 2: Project–Keep At It

One way to learn perseverance is to persevere. Here's a chance. Talk with your child about taking on a long–term project. It may take three months, six months, or it could develop into a life–long passion. Below you will find some project ideas. Use one of these, or help your child find a topic he likes better. The point is to choose something he can become passionate about. You then want to help him find lots of information. One book is not enough. Finally, he can decide what he wants to do to make a difference, to contribute to the solution of a problem, create something new, conduct an experiment, or help inform other people.

Project Idea #1—Endangered Species

Check out some of the following websites to learn more about this topic:
- http://endangered.fws.gov
- www.kidsplanet.org
- http://eelink.net/EndSpp/endangeredspecies-mainpage.html

Decide what you want to do to help:
- Start a school newspaper to tell others about endangered species.
- "Adopt" an endangered species native to your area. Find out how you can help to conserve it and inform citizens in your community about your adopted plant or animal.
- Produce public service announcements about environmental issues you care about and distribute them to the media.

Project Idea #2—Conserving Natural Resources

Check out some of the following websites to learn more about this topic:
- www.epa.gov
- www.walkerschools.org/eco
- http://water.usgs.gov/waterwatch

Decide what you want to do to help:
- Conduct a school energy audit. Brainstorm ways the school could lower energy use.
- Challenge other schools in your district to an energy conservation contest.
- Establish a school energy committee. Read energy conservation tips during morning announcements.
- Conduct a waste audit at school and identify materials that can be recycled or reused.

Persevere

Enrichment Activity

Activity 3: Project—My Heroes

Help your child identify three national heroes that overcame life challenges and persevered. Example: Michael Jordan, Walt Disney, Woodrow Wilson, etc. Cut out the frames on the next page and place a picture of each hero in one of the frames. You can search for the person's picture on the internet or your child can draw a picture or object that is associated with that person (i.e. a basketball to represent Michael Jordan). Share the heroes' challenges and achievements with friends and family.

Persevere

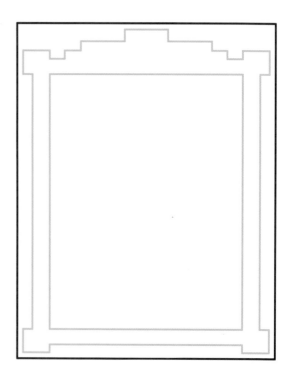

Persevere

Positive Message

Activity 4: Visual Learning

Discuss with your child the positive message below. Post the message in a visible location for your child to see it often during the month. At the end of the month, complete *Activity 5* on the other side of this sheet.

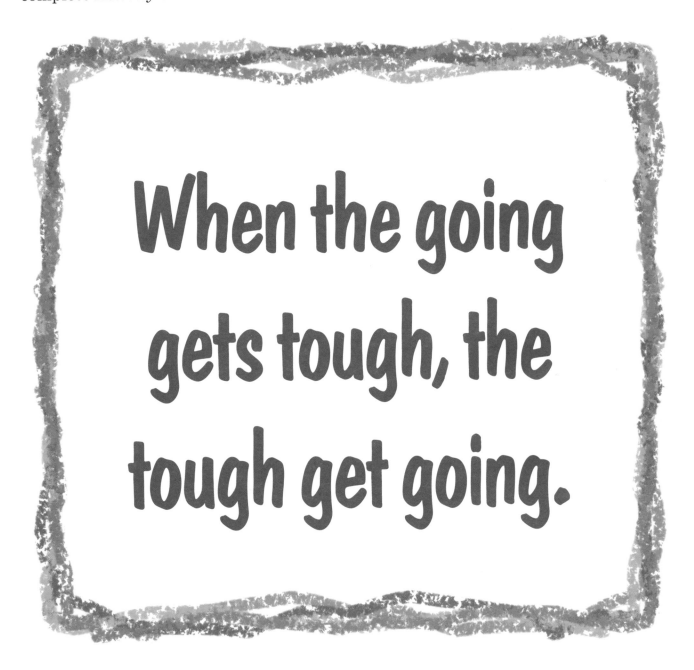

When the going gets tough, the tough get going.

Persevere

Reinforcement Activity

Activity 5: Things I Persevere At . . .

Record the things your child perseveres at and post in a visible location.

1. _____

2. _____

3. _____

4. _____

5. _____

Persevere

Reflection Activity

Activity 6: Reflection Log

Summarize your child's positive interactions during the month and reward yourself for a job well done.

Child's Name _____ **Date** _____

Name of Parent(s) _____

Record the number for each of the following questions in the box on the right.

A. How many of the workbook activities did you do with your child?

B. How many positive recognitions did your child receive from teacher(s)?

C. How many positive recognitions did your child receive from teachers, family members, friends, etc.?

D. How many positive recognitions did your child receive from you, the parent(s)?

Persevere

D. Record five self-initiated positive activities you did with your child that were not in this month's workbook activities.

1. _____

_____

2. _____

_____

3. _____

_____

4. _____

_____

5. _____

_____

Copyright© 2006 "I Care" Products & Services   (3rd Grade)

Parenting Activities

Message to Parents

Consistency is standard for many professions: writing, graphic design, food service, etc. How about professionals that rely on performance such as doctors, artists, musicians, etc. which must all perform consistently well to keep their jobs? Third grade is the time to teach consistency.

1. COMMUNICATION

What Is Consistency?

Discuss with your child the meaning of consistency—doing things regularly and the same way each time. Have her brainstorm jobs in which consistency is essential and how companies would go out of business without it. Examples could be medical labs, meat inspection, food preparation, etc.

2. ROLE PLAYING

Model It

Show your child what it means to be consistent. Examples: always enforce family rules, always be on time, don't forget to give you child his allowance, etc.

Consistency

Parenting Activities

3. TABLE TALK

Talk About It

Discuss the following with your child:

- Why would a baseball team want a player who could hit the ball consistently more than someone who occasionally slammed a home run?
- When is consistency not a good thing? (*Such as when someone is consistently wrong.*)
- What are some things that we should be consistent with?
- What are some things where consistency isn't important?

4. WRITING

Establish a Routine

Help your child learn consistency by each of you making your own "To Do" list of what needs to be done each day and each week for the entire month. Writing down activities will help you to remember to do them.

Parenting Activities

5. PHYSICAL

Test It Out

In order for a company to advertise its products as "The Best!" or "Guaranteed!," they have to know that it is better than other products and that it will do what it's supposed to every time. They determine this by doing a lot of experiments. Try the experiment on page 17 with your child to demonstrate consistency of two different kinds of paper towels.

6. READING

Practice Consistency

Take the Court by Bob Lanier and Heather Goodyear is about Li'l D and his friends who love basketball. They practice consistently until another team takes over the court. After reading the book, talk with your child about things that might make it hard for her to be consistent in doing her homework, practicing piano, getting up on time in the morning, or doing her chores. What are some of the things she can do to be more consistent?

Consistency

Parenting Activities

7. COMMUNITY

Consistency Looks Like This

Find pictures of some of the athletes in your community from the newspaper. Ask your child to explain the ways in which they have to be consistent. Provide materials so she can use the newspaper pictures to create a poster illustrating consistency. She could cut out or paint the letters of the word "consistency" and place them over the pictures. She could write a quote about consistency or let the pictures speak for themselves.

Positive Parenting Practices

- Demonstrate consistency of feelings by expressing love and acceptance to your child, even when you need to correct him.

- Set a regular time for doing homework and stick to it. Point out that consistent habits make it easier for us to be successful.

Consistency

Enrichment Activity

Activity 1: Physical—Test It Out

Materials: 10 plastic plates, 10 clear plastic cups carefully marked with a line 4 inches from the bottom and filled with water up to the line. Five cheap paper towels, five expensive paper towels, and one ruler.

Procedures: Put one paper towel in each cup of water. Transfer each paper towel to one of the plates when it has absorbed as much water as it's going to. Mark the new water line and measure how much is left in the glass. Record the results on the chart on the next page. Compare the amount of water left by the cheap paper towel to the amount of water left by the expensive paper towel. Is the more expensive paper towel more absorbent? Are the advertising claims reasonable?

Consistency

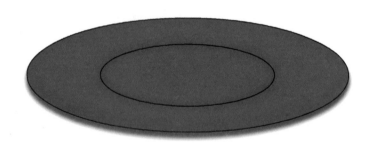

Are the Results Consistent?			
Cheap Paper Towels	**Water Left**	**Expensive Paper Towels**	**Water Left**
Towel #1		Towel #1	
Towel #2		Towel #2	
Towel #3		Towel #3	
Towel #4		Towel #4	
Towel #5		Towel #5	

Consistency

Enrichment Activity

Activity 2: Art—Practice Makes Perfect

Even artists with a lot of talent have to practice drawing to become consistently good. They might spend hours drawing the same thing over and over until they are satisfied. Have your child use the illustration on this page as a model. Draw the figure four times, once in each empty box below. Does the practice improve the drawing? Does it make sense to say that "Practice makes perfect"?

Enrichment Activity

Activity 3: Project—I Do It Consistently

Ask your child to circle the things below that she does consistently.

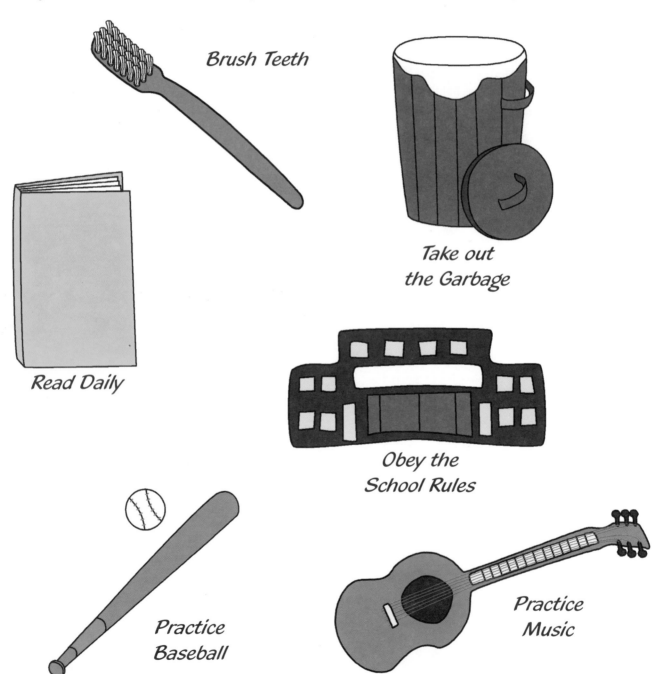

Brush Teeth

Take out
the Garbage

Read Daily

Obey the
School Rules

Practice
Baseball

Practice
Music

Copyright© 2006 "I Care" Products & Services   (3rd Grade)

Consistency

Positive Message

Activity 4: Visual Learning

Discuss with your child the positive message below. Post the message in a visible location for your child to see it often during the month. At the end of the month, complete *Activity 5* on the other side of this sheet.

The truth will always give you lasting freedom.

Consistency

Reinforcement Activity

Activity 5: Times I Have Been Consistent . . .

Record some times/situations when your child has demonstrated consistency.

1. _____

2. _____

3. _____

4. _____

5. _____

Consistency

Reflection Activity

Activity 6: Reflection Log

Summarize your child's positive interactions during the month and reward yourself for a job well done.

Child's Name _____ **Date** _____

Name of Parent(s) _____

Record the number for each of the following questions in the box on the right.

A. How many of the workbook activities did you do with your child?

B. How many positive recognitions did your child receive from teacher(s)?

C. How many positive recognitions did your child receive from teachers, family members, friends, etc.?

D. How many positive recognitions did your child receive from you, the parent(s)?

Consistency

D. Record five self–initiated positive activities you did with your child that were not in this month's workbook activities.

1. _____

   _____

2. _____

   _____

3. _____

   _____

4. _____

   _____

5. _____

   _____

Parenting Activities

Message to Parents

Dedication is recognized as one of the key elements of achievement. You can have all the talent and good ideas in the world, but without dedication, nothing will get accomplished. The good news is that dedication can be developed. It involves helping your child discover a passion and pursuing it.

1. COMMUNICATION

Why Be Dedicated?

Talk to your child about why dedication is necessary if we want to make dreams and goals come true. Ask him to decide on something he wants to be dedicated to and how he can achieve it.

2. ROLE PLAYING

Model It

Model for your child what it means to be dedicated to a positive activity. Examples could be exercise, household projects, community volunteering, etc.

Parenting Activities

3. TABLE TALK

Talk About It

Discuss the following with your child:
- Why do you think gymnastic coaches teach dedication as well as gymnastics?
- *Discuss the following quotes:* "He had a lot of talent, but not much dedication, so he failed."; "We all have dreams, but to make dreams come to life takes dedication.

4. WRITING

That's Dedication

We can recognize dedicated people. They get things done. Anyone can be dedicated to any job. You don't have to be an inventor, an artist, or a doctor. Mothers and fathers can be dedicated. So can street cleaners or restaurant chefs. If you care about doing a good job, want to help people, want to make a difference, and are willing to work, you're dedicated. Ask your child to select someone, either in history or in real life, who is dedicated. Talk about what caused that person to be dedicated and how others have benefitted from it. Have him write down the main points you have discussed.

Copyright© 2006 "I Care" Products & Services (3rd Grade)

Dedication

Parenting Activities

5. PHYSICAL

Stay Dedicated

Anyone who wants to become good at a physical activity—whether it is playing a sport, exercising, or walking every day—has to be dedicated. With your child, decide on a physical activity you will do together throughout the month. Decide on your goal. Do you want to learn a skill or spend a specified amount of time on this activity during the week? Write down your plan—who does what and when, what your reward will be if you stick to it, and who can check with you every few days to see how you're doing. Stay dedicated!

6. READING

Courage and Dedication

Harriet Tubman: Call to Freedom by Judy Carlson tells about the courage and dedication of Harriet Tubman. Determined to see her family free of slavery and help others as well, Harriet faced danger and hardship over and over again. Talk with your child about what it must have been like for Harriet. Are there any issues in life that you and your child could become dedicated to? Talk them over and decide what you could do about them.

Dedication

Parenting Activities

7. COMMUNITY

Dedicated Volunteers

Most community organizations like *The Red Cross*, *Habitat for Humanity*, or *The Cancer Society* rely on the dedication of volunteers to accomplish their goals. Select one from your community and volunteer for one day. Talk about what it takes for those who volunteer on a regular basis. Is that something you can commit to?

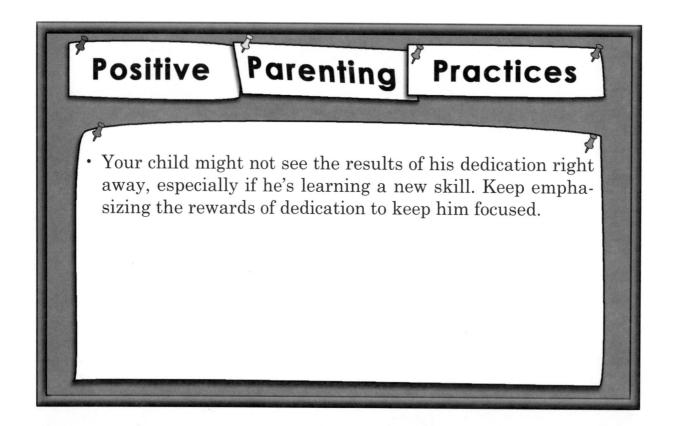

Positive Parenting Practices

- Your child might not see the results of his dedication right away, especially if he's learning a new skill. Keep emphasizing the rewards of dedication to keep him focused.

Dedication

Enrichment Activity

Activity 1: Art—It Takes Dedication to Be an Artist

Mary Cassatt was a woman whose dedication is an example for us all. She had to fight tremendous odds to become an artist in the 1880's. Read about her courage below. Then, see if you can find the video *Mary Cassatt: American Impressionist*. It's a great family movie. At the library, look for the book *Suzette and the Puppy: A Story About Mary Cassatt* by Joan Sweeney or *First Impressions: Mary Cassatt* by Susan E. Meyer. As a challenge, see if both you and your child can paint a picture in the impressionist style. It's okay to use markers.

Mary Cassatt was born in western Pennsylvania in 1844. She was one of six children. When she was seven, her family moved to France for a few years. It was there she fell in love with the paintings she saw in European museums. When her family returned to America, she decided she wanted to be an artist. That just wasn't what women did in the 19th Century. Her father even told her "I'd rather see you dead than be an artist." But he finally sent her to art school. She was made fun of by other students and when she graduated she couldn't get anyone to teach her more. Women weren't accepted as true artists. So, she moved to Paris and taught herself by copying paintings in museums. She met other painters who were not well accepted because they wanted to paint their own impression of things, not the way the art schools taught. Mary started painting her impressions as well. She was also considered different because she traveled and lived alone. Eventually her dedication paid off. Her work was eventually accepted because it was so good. Because of Mary Cassatt, respect for impressionist paintings grew and it became easier for women to become artists.

Dedication

Enrichment Activity

Activity 2: Project–Become a Collector

One of the best ways to teach dedication to your child is to help him find something to be dedicated to. Many children love collecting. With encouragement, an interest can become a passion. Does your child have collections? What might he like to collect? Some children start with toys or things they pick up outside.

Become a Collector

- *Find out all you can about your interest online or at the library.*

- *Learn about kids who collect at www.zuzu.org or search Antiques Roadshow Jr. or Smithsonian Kids.*

- *Talk to other collectors. Even if their collections are different from yours, they might have some good tips on finding objects or taking care of collections.*

- *Visit museums to see the kinds of collections they have.*

- *Go exploring to find more objects. Try flea markets, good–as–new shops, specialty stores, nature walks, fairs, conferences, etc.*

- *Learn how to care for, store, and display your collection.*

- *Share your collection with others. Create a museum at home, make a scrapbook, have a collections sharing party, etc.*

Things Kids Collect

Model cars, dolls, rocks, trains, books by a favorite author, sand, pez dispensers, candy wrappers, antiques, facts about sharks, Transformers©, figurines, pressed flowers, plates, clocks, old pictures, comics, key chains, snow globes, coins, books about horses, old cameras, stamps, poems, trading cards, stuffed animals, cats, pigs, rubber stamps, glass dogs, sports team memorabilia, pictures of all the presidents, post cards, greeting cards, stickers, wacky socks, CD's, baseball caps, clowns, Teddy bears, etc.

Dedication

Enrichment Activity

Activity 3: Art—You're Dedicated!

In Hollywood, famous people get their names, and sometimes their pictures, imprinted in a star on the sidewalk. Cut out the star below and place the picture of a dedicated friend or family member on it. Then, hang the star from the ceiling in a visible location. You can cut out the star as a template and trace it onto construction paper to create more stars if you need them.

Dedication

Cut out the star on the other side of this page
to complete the Art Activity.

Activity 4: Visual Learning

Discuss with your child the positive message below. Post the message in a visible location for your child to see it often during the month. At the end of the month, complete *Activity 5* on the other side of this sheet.

Champions are dedicated and they work hard to get things done.

Dedication

Reinforcement Activity

Activity 5: Times I Was Dedicated . . .

Record times your child was dedicated to a task or a cause and post in a visible location.

1. _____

2. _____

3. _____

4. _____

5. _____

Copyright© 2006 "I Care" Products & Services   (3rd Grade)

Dedication

Activity 6: Reflection Log

Summarize your child's positive interactions during the month and reward yourself for a job well done.

Child's Name _____ **Date** _____

Name of Parent(s) _____

Record the number for each of the following questions in the box on the right.

A. How many of the workbook activities did you do with your child?

B. How many positive recognitions did your child receive from teacher(s)?

C. How many positive recognitions did your child receive from teachers, family members, friends, etc.?

D. How many positive recognitions did your child receive from you, the parent(s)?

Dedication

D. Record five self–initiated positive activities you did with your child that were not in this month's workbook activities.

1. _____

_____

2. _____

_____

3. _____

_____

4. _____

_____

5. _____

_____

Parenting Activities

Message to Parents

In times past, strict rules of hospitality were practiced. We're more informal today, but hospitality is just as important. It represents respect for others and how thoughtful we are. People who show hospitality do have more success in life.

1. COMMUNICATION

Talk It Over

Talk with your child about the following sayings: *Do ordinary things extraordinarily well. Take care of someone like you would take care of your grandmother. Go beyond what's expected.*

2. ROLE PLAYING

Model It

Role play the following situations with your child to illustrate the difference between having manners and not having manners: receiving a gift from your grandmother, accidentally bumping into a stranger, entering the school office with a note for the secretary, thanking your friend's mother after a sleep over, opening the front door when your parents are expecting company, or any situation your child is likely to encounter.

Be Hospitable

Parenting Activities

3. TABLE TALK

Talk About It

Discuss the following with your child:

- When you want something from someone, what do you do?
- If you need help, how do you ask politely?
- Would your friends say that you are hospitable?

4. WRITING

Thank You Notes

It's a fact that successful people write thank you notes. They know the value of good manners and hospitality. They even use paper and pen, not just a quick e–mail. Purchase a box of note cards or print some out at www.kidprintables.com and link to "Thank You Cards." Your child can use them for writing thank you notes and remind her to do so. She can use the examples on page 41 to get her started.

Be Hospitable

Parenting Activities

5. PHYSICAL

In Other Cultures

The internet is making the world like one giant neighborhood. People make new friends on the other side of the globe. Did you know that there are even hospitality clubs that you can join to get to know what it's like in another country? To get a feeling for the hospitality customs of other cultures, practice some of the greetings on page 42.

6. READING

Better Manners

Read *Perfect Pigs: An Introduction to Manners* by Marc Brown. Have your child point out the situations in which she could use better manners. If she can't think of any, perhaps you can. Make a list of three or four for her to work on and ask her for a progress report weekly.

Be Hospitable

Parenting Activities

7. COMMUNITY

Customer Service

Customer service is very important to stores and restaurants. They know that if the customers are not satisfied, they will take their business elsewhere. That's why all employees are trained to be hospitable: look at, smile, and welcome a customer; ask if they can be of assistance; provide information in a pleasant manner; avoid chatting with other employees; and, above all, be sincere. As you are out in public with your child, point out examples of both good and poor customer service and discuss how the customers probably feel in each situation.

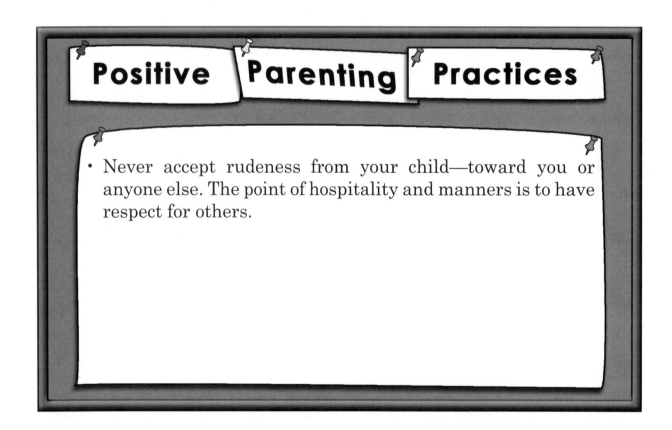

Positive Parenting Practices

- Never accept rudeness from your child—toward you or anyone else. The point of hospitality and manners is to have respect for others.

Be Hospitable

Activity 1: Writing—Thank You Notes

Use the examples below for the *Writing Activity* on page 38.

Dear Uncle Joe,
    Thank you for the catcher's mitt. It's just what I wanted. I'm on the little league team for this season. I hope you can come to a game.

                    Love,

                    Tim

Dear Hannah,
    Thank you for coming to my party. Also, thank you for the bracelet. It is very pretty.

Your Friend,

Rachel

Dear Grandma,
    Thank you for the new bedspread. It was one of my best presents. I can't wait until I see you next summer. Then, you can see how the bedspread matches my new room.
    I'm working hard in school this year. My favorite subject is language. I love to read and write poems. Thanks again for the great present! I can't wait to see you in June!

Love,

Joanne
P.S. I'm sending you one of my poems.

Be Hospitable

Enrichment Activity

Activity 2: Physical—In Other Cultures

Use the worksheet below for the *Physical Activity* on page 39.

 **Taiwan**—People greet each other by saying "Have you eaten?"

 **Morocco**—Here, people touch their heart immediately after a handshake to show that the greeting is sincere. Sometimes, instead of touching their heart, they will kiss their own hand after the handshake, as a sign of particular esteem or affection.

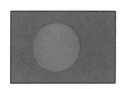 **Bangladesh**—People give each other a relaxed salute with the right hand.

 **Singapore**—Greeters put their own hands together as if they were saying a prayer, slide them backward toward their chest, and then put their hands to their heart.

 **South Africa**—They say "Howzit" which is short for "How is it?" Some will even interlock pinkies with each other, then clasp their fists, and finally interlock their pinkies again.

 **Greece**—Many people slap each other on the back instead of shaking hands.

Activity 3: Art—Table Manners Manual

Have your child make a booklet describing the table manners listed in the *Project Activity* on the next page. It could be an 8½ x 11 sheet folded in half so that it can fit next to someone's plate while they are practicing their table manners. Encourage her to be creative. She can illustrate it if she would like. This month's book *Perfect Pigs: An Introduction to Manners* by Marc Brown might give her some ideas. Once it's finished, make copies so her friends can have one when they come to dine.

Be Hospitable

Enrichment Activity

Activity 4: Project-Share the Knowledge

Help your child plan a dinner for her friends so that she can practice her hospitality and everyone can brush up on meal-time manners. You can be the coach. Go over the *Meal Time Manners* below when everyone is seated. Provide them with a copy of the manners booklet your child created in the *Art Activity*. You can begin by sharing the fact that polite people are more successful in life, starting when they are in school.

Meal Time Manners

- *Eat with a fork unless the food is meant to be eaten with fingers.*
- *Chew with your mouth closed and don't try to talk with your mouth full.*
- *Keep your elbows off the table.*
- *Don't make any rude comments about any food being served.*
- *Always say "Thank you" when you're served something.*
- *Unless you're at a buffet, wait until everyone is served and for the hostess to begin before you start eating.*
- *Eat slowly; don't gobble your food.*
- *Ask someone to pass you something that's down the table. Don't just reach for it.*
- *Put your napkin in your lap when you sit down and use it to wipe your hands or mouth if necessary.*

Be Hospitable

Activity 5: Visual Learning

Discuss with your child the positive message below. Post the message in a visible location for your child to see it often during the month. At the end of the month, complete *Activity 6* on the other side of this sheet.

Caring makes the world a kinder and gentler place to live.

Be Hospitable

Reinforcement Activity

Activity 6: When I Like to Be Hospitable . . .

Record times when your child was hospitable and post in a visible location.

1. _____

2. _____

3. _____

4. _____

5. _____

Be Hospitable

Reflection Activity

Activity 7: Reflection Log

Summarize your child's positive interactions during the month and reward yourself for a job well done.

Child's Name _____ **Date** _____

Name of Parent(s) _____

Record the number for each of the following questions in the box on the right.

A. How many of the workbook activities did you do with your child?

B. How many positive recognitions did your child receive from teacher(s)?

C. How many positive recognitions did your child receive from teachers, family members, friends, etc.?

D. How many positive recognitions did your child receive from you, the parent(s)?

Be Hospitable

D. Record five self–initiated positive activities you did with your child that were not in this month's workbook activities.

1. _____

   _____

2. _____

   _____

3. _____

   _____

4. _____

   _____

5. _____

   _____

Copyright© 2006 "I Care" Products & Services   (3rd Grade)

Parenting Activities

Message to Parents

Time is what life is made of. Unfortunately, most people take it for granted. By emphasizing punctuality and time management, you will help your child learn that by managing time wisely, he will be better able to accomplish the things that are important.

1. COMMUNICATION

If . . . Then . . .

Talk about the positive and negative consequences of punctuality. Positive: "When you have done ＿＿＿, then you can do ＿＿＿." (Example: "When you do your homework, then you can talk on the phone.") Negative: "No homework, no phone." This is also called the "If . . . Then . . . " or "Grandma's rule." Establish it as a practice in your home.

2. ROLE PLAYING

Model It

Model punctuality by arriving on time for work, appointments, and scheduled events. Keep a schedule at home as well. Have a set time for homework, meals, TV, and bedtime. It can be done with planning, even in the busiest of families, and it gives children the structure they need to function well.

Be Punctual

Parenting Activities

3. TABLE TALK

Talk About It

Discuss the following with your child:

- How long does it take you to get started on something you don't want to do?
- Does it make the job easier by putting it off?
- Why do you think people procrastinate?
- What are some of the ways you waste time?
- What does it mean to divide and conquer?

4. WRITING

Punctuality Plan

Some schools and businesses write "Punctuality Plans" to help everyone keep a schedule and be on time. As a family, sit down and talk through ways everyone can be more punctual. Having either homework or chores done before dinner might be one. Others could be laying out clothes for the next day before going to bed, using a timer to remind yourself when it is time to get off the phone, making a "To Do" list in order of importance and sticking to it, etc. Help your child turn this list into a poster that can be a reminder for the whole family.

Be Punctual

Parenting Activities

5. PHYSICAL
Try Rewards

Have you tried motivating your child to be on time with little success? Some parents find a reward system helpful. For instance, for every day that a child is ready to leave the house on time with all of his responsibilities completed, he gets a sticker on a chart. If at the end of the month he has stickers on 90% of the chart, he gets a reward. If he has stickers on less than 90%, his reward is reduced. Below 50% means no reward at all. The idea is to help your child see that punctuality has its own rewards and eventually eliminate the stickers. But you have to stick with the system for it to work.

6. READING
About Shortcuts

In *The Secret Shortcut*, by Mark Teague, Wendell and Floyd find the only way to get to school on time is to take a shortcut. After reading the book with your child, talk about shortcuts he might need to take to be punctual in getting to school, coming home from a friend's house, or getting ready for dinner. His shortcuts might involve using a watch, avoiding distractions, or setting a timer.

Be Punctual

Parenting Activities

7. COMMUNITY

What If They Were Late?

Throughout the month, carry on a discussion with your child about what would happen if various business people and service workers were late. What if doctors show up late for an operation? What if an auto mechanic decided to take the day off? What if a store manager were distracted and keeps the employees waiting for him to open the store?

Positive Parenting Practices

- Sometimes, establishing a set time, such as thirty minutes, is an effective way of encouraging kids to work quickly.
- Make the effort to always be on time for events, work, school, church, etc. Lead by example.

Be Punctual

Enrichment Activity

Activity 1: Art–Planning Guide

People learn and think differently. That means that not everyone likes using calendars and planners. But, everyone still needs to plan. Help your child design a planning guide that he will use. Look at the examples below and on the next page. Also, help him use the guide. Make copies, fill it out, and check it at the end of the day and at the end of the week. Did he follow his plans? If he didn't, why not?

Planning By Activity

Friday	
Activity	**Hours**
Sleeping	8
Getting Ready	0.5
Going to and from school	1
School	6
Planning & snack	0.5
Homework	1
Hobby (pet rabbits)	0.5
Sports	1
Play with friends	1
Dinner	0.5
Chores	0.5
TV	1.5
Reading	1
Unscheduled	1
Total	24

Monday	
Time	Activity
6 am	Get ready for school
7 am	Ride to school
8 am	School
9 am	–
10 am	–
11 am	–
12 pm	–
1 pm	–
2 pm	–
3 pm	Ride home
4 pm	Homework & snack
5 pm	Finish homework/play
6 pm	Eat dinner/Do chores
7 pm	TV
8 pm	–
9 pm	Read before bedtime
10 pm	Go to bed

Planning By Time

Be Punctual

Planning By To–Do List

Wednesday	
Priority	Activity
1	Homework
5	Research Paper
2	Soccer Practice
4	Reading for Fun
3	Wash Dishes
6	Clean Up Room

Planning By Pie Chart

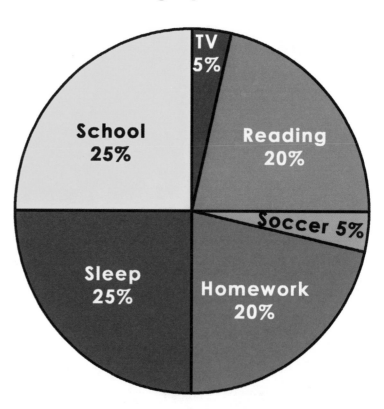

Copyright© 2006 "I Care" Products & Services   (3rd Grade)

Be Punctual

Enrichment Activity

Activity 2: Project—How Do You Spend Your Time?

You can't save time if you don't know how you're spending it. Using the charts below and on the next page, help your child keep track of his activities for several days. Concentrate on the time he has control over, such as before and between getting home from school or before going to bed. Write the number of hours he spends on each activity every day. Then, answer the questions below to see if there are ways he can save time.

Activities	Sun.	Mon.	Tue.	Wed.	Thur.	Fri.	Sat.	Total Time

1. *What did you spend the most time doing?*
2. *What did you spend the least time doing?*
3. *What would you have liked to spend more time on?*
4. *What would you have liked to spend less time on?*
5. *Were you "punctual" during the whole day? If you weren't, why not?*
6. *Was there something you didn't have time for? What? Why?*
7. *Did you do what you had decided to do? If you didn't, why not?*
8. *What are some things you can change?*
9. *How do you feel about the way you spent your time?*

Be Punctual

Time	Activity
6:00–6:30 am	
6:30–7:00 am	
7:00–7:30 am	
7:30–8:00 am	
8:00–8:30 am	
8:30–9:00 am	
9:00–9:30 am	
9:30–10:00 am	
10:00–10:30 am	
10:30–11:00 am	
11:00–11:30 am	
11:30–12:00 pm	
12:00–12:30 pm	
12:30–1:00 pm	
1:00–1:30 pm	
1:30–2:00 pm	
2:00–2:30 pm	
2:30–3:00 pm	
3:00–3:30 pm	
3:30–4:00 pm	
4:00–4:30 pm	
4:30–5:00 pm	
5:00–5:30 pm	
5:30–6:00 pm	
6:00–6:30 pm	
6:30–7:00 pm	
7:00–7:30 pm	
7:30–8:00 pm	
8:00–8:30 pm	
8:30–9:00 pm	
9:00–9:30 pm	
9:30–10:00 pm	

Time	Activity
6:00–6:30 am	
6:30–7:00 am	
7:00–7:30 am	
7:30–8:00 am	
8:00–8:30 am	
8:30–9:00 am	
9:00–9:30 am	
9:30–10:00 am	
10:00–10:30 am	
10:30–11:00 am	
11:00–11:30 am	
11:30–12:00 pm	
12:00–12:30 pm	
12:30–1:00 pm	
1:00–1:30 pm	
1:30–2:00 pm	
2:00–2:30 pm	
2:30–3:00 pm	
3:00–3:30 pm	
3:30–4:00 pm	
4:00–4:30 pm	
4:30–5:00 pm	
5:00–5:30 pm	
5:30–6:00 pm	
6:00–6:30 pm	
6:30–7:00 pm	
7:00–7:30 pm	
7:30–8:00 pm	
8:00–8:30 pm	
8:30–9:00 pm	
9:00–9:30 pm	
9:30–10:00 pm	

Be Punctual

Activity 4: Visual Learning

Discuss with your child the positive message below. Post the message in a visible location for your child to see it often during the month. At the end of the month, complete *Activity 5* on the other side of this sheet.

Being on time is one way to show respect to others.

Be Punctual

Reinforcement Activity

Activity 5: I Am Punctual When I . . .

Record examples of times when your child was punctual and post in a visible location.

1. _____

2. _____

3. _____

4. _____

5. _____

Be Punctual

Reflection Activity

Activity 6: Reflection Log

Summarize your child's positive interactions during the month and reward yourself for a job well done.

Child's Name _____ **Date** _____

Name of Parent(s) _____

Record the number for each of the following questions in the box on the right.

A. How many of the workbook activities did you do with your child? ☐

B. How many positive recognitions did your child receive from teacher(s)? ☐

C. How many positive recognitions did your child receive from teachers, family members, friends, etc.? ☐

D. How many positive recognitions did your child receive from you, the parent(s)? ☐

Be Punctual

D. Record five self–initiated positive activities you did with your child that were not in this month's workbook activities.

1. _____

   _____

2. _____

   _____

3. _____

   _____

4. _____

   _____

5. _____

   _____

Parenting Activities

Message to Parents

Gentleness is not weakness, cowardice, or passivity. It is strength. It is choosing to be sensitive to how other people feel and what they need. It offers assurance and helps people develop trust and confidence.

1. COMMUNICATION

What Is Gentleness?

Talk with your child about what gentleness is. You can use some of these examples: making it safe for people and animals to be around you; touching carefully; speaking with a soft voice; sharing your feelings peacefully; moving slowly; showing sensitivity, consideration, and respect; etc.

2. ROLE PLAYING

Model It

How comfortable are you with gentleness? With speaking softly and taking time with people? Of talking things out peacefully? Are you respectful of your child? Stay alert to how your child perceives you. You can set guidelines and can discipline your child while still being gentle.

Be Gentle

Parenting Activities

3. TABLE TALK

Talk About It

Discuss the following with your child:
- Why is it good to let someone else go first?
- What does it mean if someone tells you that you're very considerate?
- Why do you think it's important to be gentle?
- How can you be gentle with yourself?

4. WRITING

I Am Gentle

Help your child create an acrostic poem with her name and words or phrases that describe how gentle she is. See page 65 to view an example and to learn more about acrostic poems.

Be Gentle

Parenting Activities

5. PHYSICAL

Doing Things

Doing things for others can help children develop a sense of caring and the desire to do things, not for a reward, but because they are helpful and right. Have your child make heart–shaped pretzels using the recipe on page 66. Have her wrap each in cellophane with a bow and give it to someone special.

6. READING

Being More Gentle

Amber is a little upset. Her parents just got a divorce and they spend more time fussing about each other than thinking about Amber's feelings. Read *Amber Brown Sees Red*, by Paula Danziger, then talk about some of the ways the people in your family could be more gentle with each other.

Be Gentle

Parenting Activities

7. COMMUNITY

Sharing With Others

Talk with your child about the importance of caring for those in need—especially other children. Have her go through her toys and select three or four to donate. Make sure the toys are not broken and encourage her to donate one toy she really likes. The local *Red Cross* or *Salvation Army* can tell you where to take them. She could even encourage her friends to do the same.

Positive Parenting Practices

- Expose your child to other people who are kind and caring so that she will have several role models.

- Make the effort to always talk to your child in a soft, encouraging tone of voice.

Be Gentle

Enrichment Activity

Activity 1: Writing—Writing Acrostic Poems

An acrostic poem is a poem where the first letters of the first word in each line spell another word when read down. Also, each line of the poem usually describes that word. Review the instructions and examples below.

1. Write your name down a piece of paper.
2. Make a list of all the ways that you are gentle. Don't try to only think of words that begin with the letters in your name, list anything you think of. You can make the words or ideas fit later.
3. Look through the list of ideas you wrote down. If the idea you want to put into the poem doesn't begin with the letters found in the subject word, think of how that word could be put into a sentence that begins with a letter from the subject word.

Devoted,
On
Guard.

Jolly,
Outgoing,
Excellent.

Loves hamburgers
Usually
Insists on
Silly and cool games.

Delightful,
Obedient,
Good.

Green grass grows in the summer.
Really good apples are green.
Even a marker is green.
Even a frog is very dark green.
New green backpacks are cool for school.

Be Gentle

Parenting Activities

Activity 2: Physical-Gentle Pretzels

Recipe for Homemade Pretzels

2   16 oz. loaves of frozen bread dough
1   egg white, slightly beaten
1   teaspoon water
     Coarse salt

Thaw the bread dough and make about 20 balls of equal size, about 1 ½ inches each. Roll each of the balls into a rope about 12 inches long. Have your child twist the rope into hearts or other shapes. Put the pretzels one inch apart on a greased cookie sheet and let them stand for 20 minutes. Then, brush them with the combined egg white and water and sprinkle the top of each with course salt. Place them on the middle rack of the oven that's been preheated to 350°. Put a broiling pan with about 1 inch of water on the bottom rack of the oven. Bake for 20 minutes or until golden brown.

Be Gentle

Enrichment Activity

Activity 3: Art—Pictures of Gentleness

Many artists create pictures that express gentleness. Check out some of the websites below to find some examples your child likes. Then, have her create her own picture of gentleness.

- www.brendaharristustian.com

- http://eu.easyart.com (Search for *Anne Gardner*)

- http://www.naturalchild.com/gallery/home.html

Activity 4: Project—Make a Difference

Help your child recognize how one simple act of kindness can make a difference in someone's life. Have your child decorate several small flower pots by pasting pictures on them or painting them. Then, fill the flower pots with soil and plant a few flower seeds in each. Give her the responsibility for caring for the plants and following the directions on the seed packet. When the flowers have begun to sprout, arrange for your child to take them to a nursing home and personally give each pot to a different resident.

Be Gentle

Activity 5: Discussion–Gentleness

Discuss with your child how the things below can be used to show gentleness.

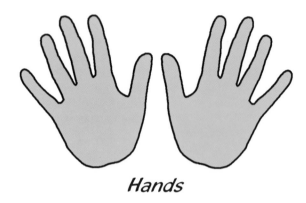

Hands

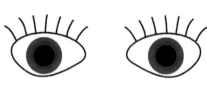

Eyes

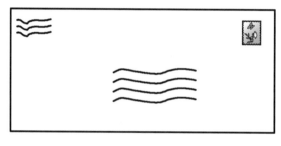

Letter

Smile

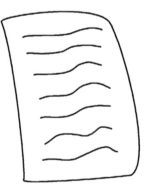

Poem

Copyright© 2006 "I Care" Products & Services   (3rd Grade)

Be Gentle

Positive Message

Activity 6: Visual Learning

Discuss with your child the positive message below. Post the message in a visible location for your child to see it often during the month. At the end of the month, complete *Activity 7* on the other side of this sheet.

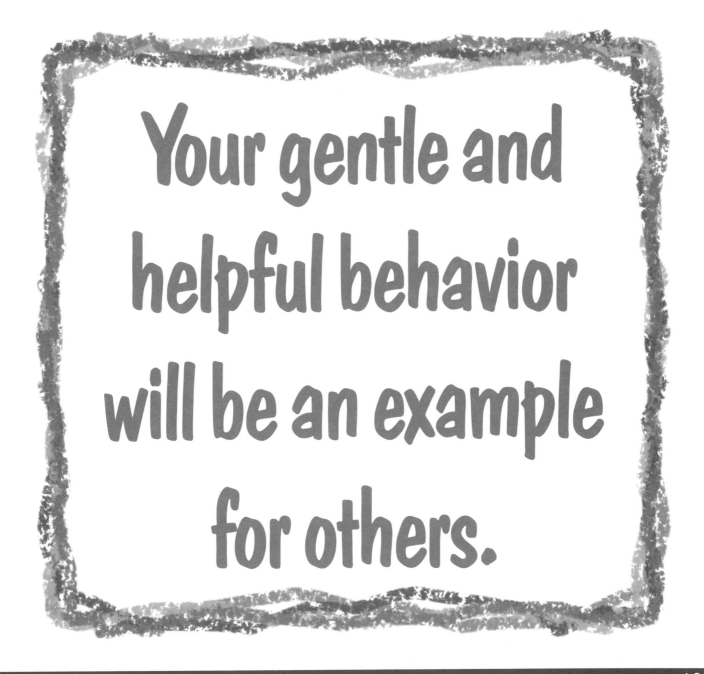

Your gentle and helpful behavior will be an example for others.

Be Gentle

Reinforcement Activity

Activity 7: Being Gentle With Others . . .

Record examples of times your child was gentle with others and post in a visible location.

1. _____

2. _____

3. _____

4. _____

5. _____

Copyright© 2006 "I Care" Products & Services   (3rd Grade)

Be Gentle

Reflection Activity

Activity 8: Reflection Log

Summarize your child's positive interactions during the month and reward yourself for a job well done.

Child's Name _____ **Date** _____

Name of Parent(s) _____

Record the number for each of the following questions in the box on the right.

A. How many of the workbook activities did you do with your child?

B. How many positive recognitions did your child receive from teacher(s)?

C. How many positive recognitions did your child receive from teachers, family members, friends, etc.?

D. How many positive recognitions did your child receive from you, the parent(s)?

Be Gentle

D. Record five self-initiated positive activities you did with your child that were not in this month's workbook activities.

1. _____

_____

2. _____

_____

3. _____

_____

4. _____

_____

5. _____

_____

Copyright© 2006 "I Care" Products & Services   (3rd Grade)

The Value of Prudence

Parenting Activities

Message to Parents

Prudence is using good judgment. With all of the choices available to children today and the pressure from media and peers, children need prudence. They learn it best by seeing it in action.

1. COMMUNICATION

Here's What I Did

Talk to your child about situations in which you used good judgment and what happened as a result. Examples: you told your teacher when a classmate tried to get you to misbehave and she moved your seat; you stopped listening to music while doing your homework which made it possible to finish much faster; etc.

2. ROLE PLAYING

Model It

Be a model of prudent spending by not purchasing a lot of unnecessary items if you have financial obligations. Point out how people get into debt if they overspend and why that is not being prudent.

The Value of Prudence

Parenting Activities

3. TABLE TALK

Talk About It

Discuss the following with your child:

- *Help your child decide the wisest response to the following situations:* What would you do if, when you got home, no one was there and you didn't have a key?; What if several classmates wouldn't stop teasing you?; What if there were a strange dog walking toward you and no one else was around?

- *Ask your child to share his thoughts on the following sayings:* "Look before you leap."; "Think before you act."

4. WRITING

Household Dangers

Help your child create a pamphlet for kids about household dangers. What are they? How does one avoid them? What do you do if someone gets hurt? Having information will help children make wise decisions when the time comes. To get started, look at the example on page 77.

The Value of Prudence

Parenting Activities

5. PHYSICAL

What Would You Do?

Talk over with your child when you might use some of the following responses. (1) I chose the game, so you go first. (2) Let's decide on the rules and shake on them. (3) I want to hear both sides of the story first. (4) Let's find a way to make things fair. (5) Let's take turns. You go first. (6) That's not fair. You're not treating him right. Then, pick several situations he is likely to encounter, such as taking turns or playing with someone who doesn't follow the rules. Have him act out the situations and respond in a cooperative way.

6. READING

Wisdom and Courage

Felicity Saves the Day, by Valerie Tripp, is about a young girl whose wisdom and courage not only save the day, but also save the runaway apprentice who has fled to join the Colonial Army of the Revolutionary War. Read this book with your child and enjoy Felicity's adventure. You will also learn about life in 1774. Then, talk with your child about ways he can help others in need.

The Value of Prudence

Parenting Activities

7. COMMUNITY

Save the Planet

Discuss with your child why a healthy environment is prudent. Have him identify and carry out a project to contribute to a healthy environment. Examples: collecting litter, writing ads to encourage recycling, planting a tree, beautifying the neighborhood, etc.

Positive Parenting Practices

• Catch your child using good judgment and praise him for it. Examples: saving money, doing homework without being reminded, picking friends who will be a good influence.

• Children's brains are still developing. They are not as good as adults in knowing where sounds come from, seeing out of the corner of their eyes, or putting all the facts together in an emergency. That means that no matter what we teach them, we are still responsible for their safety.

The Value of Prudence

Enrichment Activity

Activity 1: Writing—Making a Pamphlet

These tips work whether you use a computer or print it by hand.

- *A pamphlet can be a piece of 8½ x 11 paper folded in half or into three panels.*

- *Keep the message you want to share brief. Only tell about that.*

- *You should have an interesting headline to get people's attention on each panel or page.*

- *The best pamphlets are short and simple. You can use bullets to list things, so you don't have to use paragraphs.*

- *Leave some space in between the writing, either as empty white space or as space for logos or pictures. This makes it easier for people to read.*

- *Use interesting fonts.*

- *Check your spelling.*

- *Make copies on a copier and fold them.*

The Value of Prudence

Enrichment Activity

Activity 2: Art—"Yellow Light" Feelings

Sometimes children will say more in drawings than to you directly. Ask your child to identify three things that give him that "yellow light" feeling: situations that give him a funny feeling in his tummy or make him nervous or unsafe, then have him draw them. Later, sit down and talk about the drawings, his feelings and what he can do in each situation to feel safe. Situations might be coming home to an empty house or talking in front of a group of strangers.

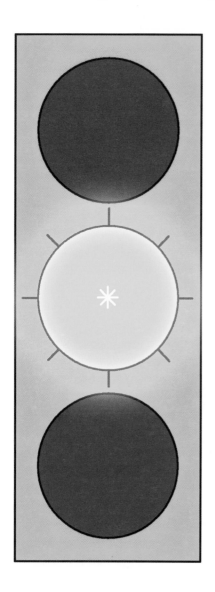

Copyright© 2006 "I Care" Products & Services   (3rd Grade)

The Value of Prudence

Enrichment Activity

Activity 3: Project—Spending Money Wisely

Help your child establish the habit of saving money each time he gets his allowance. Discuss how the accumulated money can be spent on something he wants, then help him set up a spending plan like the one below.

Spending Rules:
- *Save 10% for a new bike*
- *Plan for what I have to buy myself*
- *Buy what I need before buying what I want*
- *Save for something special*

My income this week: _____

How much do I have to spend? _____

How much will lunch cost? _____

How much do I want to save for a new video game? _____

How much do I want to spend on treats? _____

Total Used: _____

Money left over: _____

Activity 4: Project-Evaluation "T"

On the left side of the "T" below, list the advantages of playing sports and on the right side of the "T," list the disadvantages of playing sports. After both sides are filled in, discuss which choice, either to play sports or not to play sports, would be the most prudent, or wisest, choice.

Would it be prudent to play sports?

Advantages	Disadvantages

The Value of Prudence

Activity 5: Visual Learning

Discuss with your child the positive message below. Post the message in a visible location for your child to see it often during the month. At the end of the month, complete *Activity 6* on the other side of this sheet.

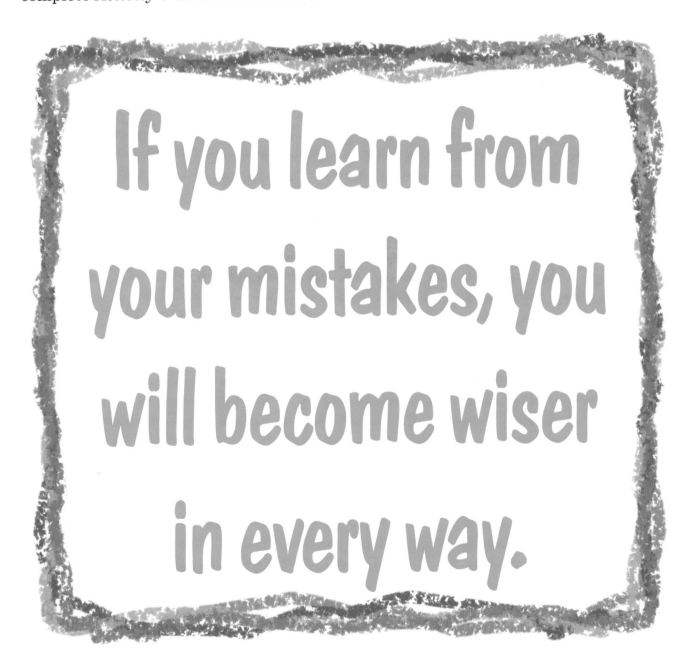

If you learn from your mistakes, you will become wiser in every way.

The Value of Prudence

Reinforcement Activity

Activity 6: I Am Prudent When . . .

Record examples of when your child demonstrated prudence and post in a visible location.

1. _____

2. _____

3. _____

4. _____

5. _____

Copyright© 2006 "I Care" Products & Services   (3rd Grade)

The Value of Prudence

Reflection Activity

Activity 7: Reflection Log

Summarize your child's positive interactions during the month and reward yourself for a job well done.

Child's Name _____ **Date** _____

Name of Parent(s) _____

Record the number for each of the following questions in the box on the right.

A. How many of the workbook activities did you do with your child? ☐

B. How many positive recognitions did your child receive from teacher(s)? ☐

C. How many positive recognitions did your child receive from teachers, family members, friends, etc.? ☐

D. How many positive recognitions did your child receive from you, the parent(s)? ☐

The Value of Prudence

D. Record five self–initiated positive activities you did with your child that were not in this month's workbook activities.

1. _____

   _____

2. _____

   _____

3. _____

   _____

4. _____

   _____

5. _____

   _____

Understand Consequences

Parenting Activities

Message to Parents

Because our brains aren't fully developed until the age of 21 or 22, children cannot always reason clearly. However, knowing the possible consequences of their actions will help them make good decisions.

1. COMMUNICATION

Is It Worth It?

Talk with your child about the difference between short– and long–term consequences. An action may seem positive if the immediate effect is good, but if you look at the longer–term consequences, the action may not be worthwhile at all. For instance, it might be fun to stay home from school, but having to make up the work later isn't worth it. Also, talk about actions that have good long–term consequences, but may not seem very positive at the moment. A good example is the hard work that goes into learning to play the piano, being a really good gymnast, or learning a language.

2. ROLE PLAYING

Model It

As you go through the month, dialogue with your child about the consequences of some of the things you do. An example could be not having enough money for a special purchase because you spent it on something you didn't need. The lesson learned is to budget ahead of time. Another example could be forgetting to pick up a grocery item which meant you had to make another trip to the store. The lesson learned is to make a shopping list.

Understand Consequences

Parenting Activities

3. TABLE TALK

Talk About It

Discuss the following with your child:

- What are the consequences to the following? (1) That list of vocabulary words is so long that I think I'll copy it tomorrow. (2) I really studied hard for the test. (3) The new boy in class is getting teased a lot. (4) I wasn't paying attention when they told us we needed to dress up for the field trip.
- If you had to make a hard decision, why would it be important to think about it awhile instead of doing something quickly?
- What should be the consequences if . . .

4. WRITING

The Day I Didn't Obey

Ask your child to share a lesson she learned from not obeying you. What were the consequences? Have her write about it and share her story with the family.

Understand Consequences

5. PHYSICAL

Know the Consequences

It's not too early to begin talking to your child about the consequences of taking drugs. At this age, they can relate to the physical consequences better than to the effects on thinking and emotions. Review some of the facts on page 89. You can find additional resources online or through your child's school.

6. READING

Unintended Consequences

When you read *King Midas and the Golden Touch*, as told by Charlotte Craft, notice how well the illustrator has shown the pleasure and pain of the characters. Then, talk about how painful it can be to suffer unintended consequences, just as King Midas did.

Understand Consequences

Parenting Activities

7. COMMUNITY

Follow the Rules

Go over the rules your child is expected to follow at school, on the bus, in class, at the cafeteria, on the playground, etc. Discuss each set of rules and the consequences that would follow if the rules were broken. What positive consequences occur when the rules are followed?

Positive Parenting Practices

- Natural consequences are a powerful teaching tool. If your child rides his bike when he should be studying, his bike riding privilege should be suspended. If he breaks something, he has to earn money to replace it. If he refuses to pick up his toys, the toys are put away for a week.

Copyright© 2006 "I Care" Products & Services   (3rd Grade)

Understand Consequences

Activity 1: Physical-Know the Consequences

Things you sniff and smell

Short–Term—sneezing, lack of coordination, loss of appetite, rapid heart-beat, seizures, confusion, and impulsive behavior that may lead to injuries and accidents

Long–Term—nosebleeds, loss of consciousness, hepatitis, liver failure, kidney failure, trouble breathing, irregular heartbeat, and possible suffocation

Alcohol

Short–Term—lack of concentration, weak muscles, too much at once can cause unconsciousness or even death from respiratory paralysis

Long–Term—liver failure and death.

Narcotics

Short–Term—skin abscesses, inability to go to the bathroom, nausea, and respiratory depression

Long–Term—sickness if you try to stop taking them

Understand Consequences

Enrichment Activity

Activity 2: Project—Think It Through

One way to make good decisions is to think about the good and the bad that would happen as a result of the decision. Help your child use a "T–Chart" to examine the good and bad of "What would happen if there were no more tests in school?" and "What happens when you argue with your parents?" Then, look in the newspapers for examples in your community of people who probably didn't make very good decisions. What were the consequences?

What would happen if there were no more tests in school?

Good	Bad
• Kids wouldn't get nervous because a test was coming up.	• It would be harder for teachers to know how much kids had learned.
• Teachers would have to find other ways to see what kids had learned.	• It would be harder to give out grades.
	• It would be harder to know who should go on to the next grade.

Understand Consequences

What happens when you argue with your parents?

Good	Bad

Enrichment Activity

Activity 3: Art–Picture It

Have your child illustrate several situations in which someone has to deal with the consequences of his behavior. Examples might include a boy forgets to look before crossing the street, parents leave dangerous cleaning liquids within reach of young children, someone forgets to fasten the screen door and the dog gets out, some classmates are gossiping about a new student, etc.

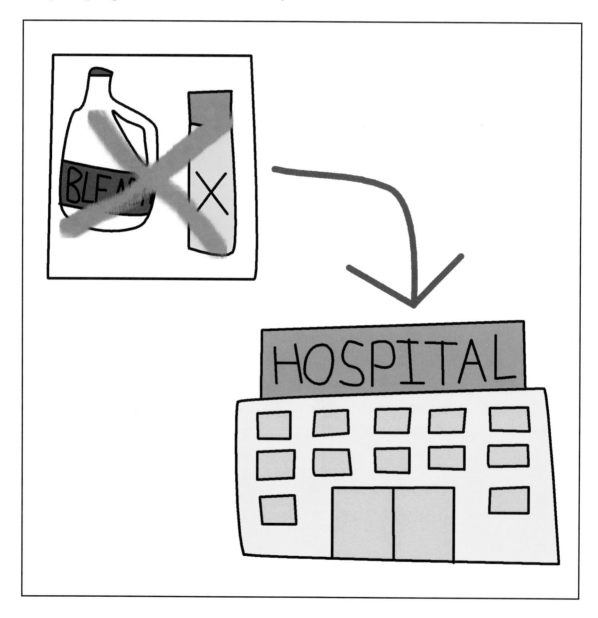

Understand Consequences

Activity 4: Visual Learning

Discuss with your child the positive message below. Post the message in a visible location for your child to see it often during the month. At the end of the month, complete *Activity 5* on the other side of this sheet.

Taking responsibility for your mistakes is a strength, not a weakness.

Understand Consequences

Reinforcement Activity

Activity 5: Understanding Consequences

Record the consequences of some of your child's actions and post in a visible location.

1. _____

2. _____

3. _____

4. _____

5. _____

Copyright© 2006 "I Care" Products & Services   (3rd Grade)

Understand Consequences

Reflection Activity

Activity 6: Reflection Log

Summarize your child's positive interactions during the month and reward yourself for a job well done.

Child's Name _____ **Date** _____

Name of Parent(s) _____

Record the number for each of the following questions in the box on the right.

A. How many of the workbook activities did you do with your child?

B. How many positive recognitions did your child receive from teacher(s)?

C. How many positive recognitions did your child receive from teachers, family members, friends, etc.?

D. How many positive recognitions did your child receive from you, the parent(s)?

Understand Consequences

D. Record five self–initiated positive activities you did with your child that were not in this month's workbook activities.

1. _____

_____

2. _____

_____

3. _____

_____

4. _____

_____

5. _____

_____

The Value of Being Alert

Parenting Activities

Message to Parents

Being alert means paying attention to what is happening around you. That involves both observation and instinct. Help your child become more alert by pointing out your own observations on a regular basis and asking him to share his own.

1. COMMUNICATION

Day Dreaming

Read with your child the *Aesop Fable* entitled *The Milkmaid and Her Pail* on page 101. Talk with him about the consequences of not staying alert. Has he ever done the wrong homework assignment, missed the school bus because he wasn't paying attention to the time, messed up an assignment because he didn't read the instructions, or shown up at a friend's house at the wrong time? You can even discuss the importance of alertness for different professions and jobs, such as doctors, assembly line workers, pilots, etc.

2. ROLE PLAYING

Model It

It's a fact that kids who watch TV or use the computer a lot are less alert and thus perform more poorly in school. Model healthy living. Drinking plenty of water, eating right, and exercising all contribute to healthy alertness. Then, use self–talk (talking out loud to yourself) to show your child how careful you are while driving, using power tools, or doing anything else that requires your careful attention.

The Value of Being Alert

Parenting Activities

3. TABLE TALK

Talk About It

Discuss the following with your child:

- *Referring to the motto "Stay alert. Stay safe," review safety rules for crossing the street, bike riding, household poisons, strange animals, etc.*
- *Ask your child if he's noticed anything different about _____ .*
- *Check on your child's alertness at school by asking questions that require observation:* What color was the sweater your teacher was wearing? How many messages from the office did you have today? What did you have for lunch today? What did you play at recess? What did you talk about with your friends?, etc. *Do this daily for a week to see if his alertness increases over the week.*

4. WRITING

Are You Alert?

Alert means paying close attention. It also refers to being awake enough to pay attention. Make sure your child is awake enough to keep alert during the day. Research says that 6 to 9–year–olds need 10 hours of sleep every night. Every school day for a week, have your child write down the number of hours of sleep he gets and how alert he feels the next morning. At the end of the week, ask him to write about whether he was more alert when he got more sleep. He can use the chart on page 102 for record keeping.

The Value of Being Alert

5. PHYSICAL

Watch Carefully

Play games with your child that require him to be alert. Examples: kite flying, remote control cars, video games, juggling, concentration or other card games that require remembering what cards were shown previously, etc. What happens when he doesn't pay attention?

6. READING

Safety Tips

Who Is a Stranger and What Should I Do? by Linda W. Girard is full of information and safety tips to help your child to stay alert and avoid being a victim. Read the book through several times and periodically review the procedures. Remind your child that he can use the tips with anyone who makes him uncomfortable. It's often people we know who abuse children.

The Value of Being Alert

Parenting Activities

7. COMMUNITY

Project Protect

With the help of neighborhood parents, decide what you'd want your children to do in the case of emergencies. Have a meeting where parents and children talk about the rules. This way, the children can see that there are other adults who are interested in their safety. On page 103, you'll find some of the things other parents have done.

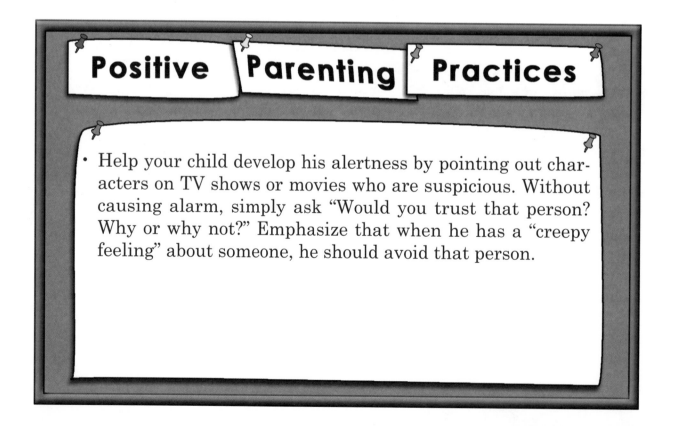

Positive Parenting Practices

- Help your child develop his alertness by pointing out characters on TV shows or movies who are suspicious. Without causing alarm, simply ask "Would you trust that person? Why or why not?" Emphasize that when he has a "creepy feeling" about someone, he should avoid that person.

September
The Value of Being Alert

Activity 1: Communication—Aesop's Fable

The Milkmaid and Her Pail
by
Aesop

Patty the Milkmaid was going to market carrying her milk in a pail on her head. As she went along, she began calculating what she would do with the money she would get for the milk.

"I'll buy some fowls from Farmer Brown," she said, "and they will lay eggs each morning, which I will sell to the parson's wife. With the money that I get from the sale of these eggs, I'll buy myself a new dimity frock and a chip hat; and when I go to market, won't all the young men come up and speak to me! Polly Shaw will be jealous, but I don't care. I shall just look at her and toss my head like this."

As she spoke, she tossed her head back, the pail fell off of it, and all the milk was spilled. So, she had to go home and tell her mother what had happened.

"Ah, my child," said the mother, "Do not count your chickens before they are hatched."

The Value of Being Alert

Enrichment Activity

Activity 2: Writing–Staying Alert

Use the chart below for the *Writing Activity* on page 98.

Does Getting More Sleep Help Me Stay Alert?

Hours of Sleep	How Alert I Felt the Next Day
Day 1:	
Day 2:	
Day 3:	
Day 4:	
Day 5:	
Day 6:	
Day 7:	

Activity 3: Community-Project Protect

Use the information below for the *Community Activity* on page 100.

Keeping Kids Safe

Over the last 25 years, neighborhood watches and block parent programs have been established throughout the country. Some programs are very organized and provide training for parents and other neighborhood volunteers. Some are informal groups of parents who agree to be available at specified times—primarily before and after school—for children to go to in times of distress, such as being lost, being bothered by strangers, being sick or injured, losing a house key, being caught in bad weather, etc. Parents contact the proper authorities or the parents as the situation requires. They don't administer first aid, provide food, drink, medicine, or transportation, nor do they provide restrooms.

For more information, you can log on to the following websites:
- www.loveourchildrenusa.org (link to *Block Parents*)
- www.find-missing-children.org/Safety
- www.find-missing-children.org (link to *Safety Tips*)

The Value of Being Alert

Enrichment Activity

Activity 4: Art—Comic Strip

Create a comic strip to tell a story about what happens when you don't stay alert. Use the planning sheet on the next page or go to www.garfield.com and link to *Fun 'n' Games*, then *Comic Creator* or to www.snoopy.com to get some ideas. You can cut out the comic strips and post them in a visible location.

WHAT I WANT IN MY COMIC STRIP:

BACKGROUND—KEEP IT SIMPLE

CHARACTERS—TWO OR THREE AT MOST

ACTION—HAS TO BE SHOWN IN THREE OR FOUR FRAMES

CAPTIONS—SHORT AND SIMPLE

HINT: IN GARFIELD COMICS, SOMETIMES THE ONLY CHANGE FROM ONE FRAME TO THE NEXT IS THE EXPRESSION ON GARFIELD'S FACE.

The Value of Being Alert

Cut out the comic strips on the other side of this page and display them for the Art Activity

The Value of Being Alert

Positive Message

Activity 3: Visual Learning

Discuss with your child the positive message below. Post the message in a visible location for your child to see it often during the month. At the end of the month, complete *Activity 4* on the other side of this sheet.

Staying alert will help you do things well and on time. It will also help you stay safe.

The Value of Being Alert

Reinforcement Activity

Activity 4: Being Alert

Record some times your child demonstrated alertness and post in a visible location.

1. _____

2. _____

3. _____

4. _____

5. _____

The Value of Being Alert

Reflection Activity

Activity 5: Reflection Log

Summarize your child's positive interactions during the month and reward yourself for a job well done.

Child's Name _____ **Date** _____

Name of Parent(s) _____

Record the number for each of the following questions in the box on the right.

A. How many of the workbook activities did you do with your child? ☐

B. How many positive recognitions did your child receive from teacher(s)? ☐

C. How many positive recognitions did your child receive from teachers, family members, friends, etc.? ☐

D. How many positive recognitions did your child receive from you, the parent(s)? ☐

The Value of Being Alert

D. Record five self–initiated positive activities you did with your child that were not in this month's workbook activities.

1. _____

   _____

2. _____

   _____

3. _____

   _____

4. _____

   _____

5. _____

   _____

Have Courage

Parenting Activities

Message to Parents

Practice will help you prepare children to be courageous. Giving them opportunities to think through decisions in advance, to say no with confidence, or to overcome something that makes them nervous is important.

---

1. COMMUNICATION

Courage Is . . .

Talk with your child about how courage is doing something we're scared to do. Share situations in which you have overcome your fear with courage. Ask your child something it would take courage for her to do and how she can overcome her fear.

2. ROLE PLAYING

Model It

When you see examples of courage during the month, even in yourself, be sure to point them out to your child. Any situation qualifies in which someone did the right thing, despite the difficulties.

111

Have Courage

Parenting Activities

3. TABLE TALK

Talk About It

Discuss the following with your child:

- *Ask your child to complete the following sentence, giving as many reasons as possible: "I'm brave because I _____ ." Examples: try new things, tell myself how brave I am, stand up to bullies, etc.*
- *Discuss with your child how it sometimes takes courage to say "No" when friends want to break the rules. Practice with her how to politely say "No" to different situations.*

4. WRITING

Why Mosquitoes Buzz in Ears

"Pour Quoi Stories" explain why things happen, like the West African story of "Why Mosquitoes Buzz in People's Ears." You can search "Pour Quoi Stories" on the internet or in the local library. After reading a few together, you and your child can each write a story about courage. You'll need to decide what you are explaining, who your characters are, what the setting is, and what happens.

Have Courage

Parenting Activities

5. PHYSICAL

Practicing Courage

Plan an outing with your child to do something that will take courage. Examples could be climbing a rock wall; trying a new sport; participating in a drama, music, or dance program; etc.

6. READING

Overcoming Fear

Stories of great courage get passed from generation to generation. *Call It Courage*, by Armstrong Sperry, is one of these stories. After reading it with your child, talk about how Mafatu was able to overcome his fear and prove himself courageous. Does your child have some fears? Talk about how she can conquer them.

Parenting Activities

7. COMMUNITY

Examples of Courage

Assist your child in finding stories in your local newspaper about people who have shown great courage. Make a "courage collage" using these pictures and articles. It might feature doctors, rescue workers, policemen and women, volunteers, or anyone else whose job requires courage.

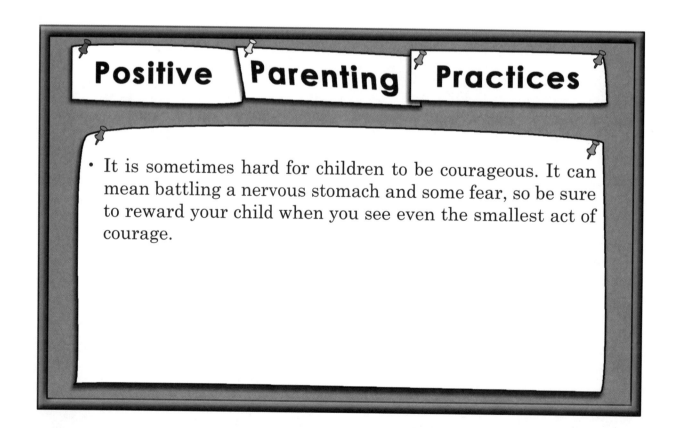

Positive Parenting Practices

- It is sometimes hard for children to be courageous. It can mean battling a nervous stomach and some fear, so be sure to reward your child when you see even the smallest act of courage.

Enrichment Activity

Activity 1: Project–Overcoming Fear

Share with your child the fact that talking in front of people is the biggest fear most people have. Over the next month, help her develop her courage for speaking in front of groups by doing the activities described on this page.

Developing Courage to Speak in Front of Groups

These activities are designed to help your child to become more comfortable speaking in front of groups. Space them out over the next month, doing one every 5 to 7 days.

1. Read aloud to your family. How about the story of Amelia Earhart or Clara Barton, both women of courage. Other possibilities are Martin Luther King, Jr., Ceasar Chavez, and Abraham Lincoln. Biographies of courageous people are available at the public library.

2. Retell the story of Mafatu after you've read the book *Call It Courage*. All you have to do is tell the main points in your own words.

3. Memorize the quotes on courage on the next page and recite them to your family. Stand up and look at them when you do. You may even want to share the quotes with your class at school.

Have Courage

"To go against what your friends think is perhaps the most difficult act of courage you can perform."—Author Unknown

"To know what is right and not to do it is the worst cowardice."—Confucius

"Keep your fears to yourself, but share your courage with others."—Robert Louis Stevenson

"Courage doesn't always roar. Sometimes courage is a little voice at the end of the day that says 'I'll try again tomorrow.'"—Mary Anne Radmacher

"Courage is what it takes to stand up and speak; courage is also what it takes to sit down and listen."—Winston Churchill

"We must build dikes of courage to hold back the flood of fear."—Martin Luther King, Jr.

"Courage is found in unlikely places."—J. R. R. Tolkien

Have Courage

Enrichment Activity

Activity 2: Art—Medal of Courage

Police and fire departments award medals of courage to people who have done exceptional acts of bravery. Help your child design and make a medal of courage to give to someone she considers especially brave, someone who stood up for what he believed. She can use the template on the next page to get her started. She can even have an awards ceremony by planning a special meal and inviting that person. If the person isn't local, send the medal to him or her through the mail.

117

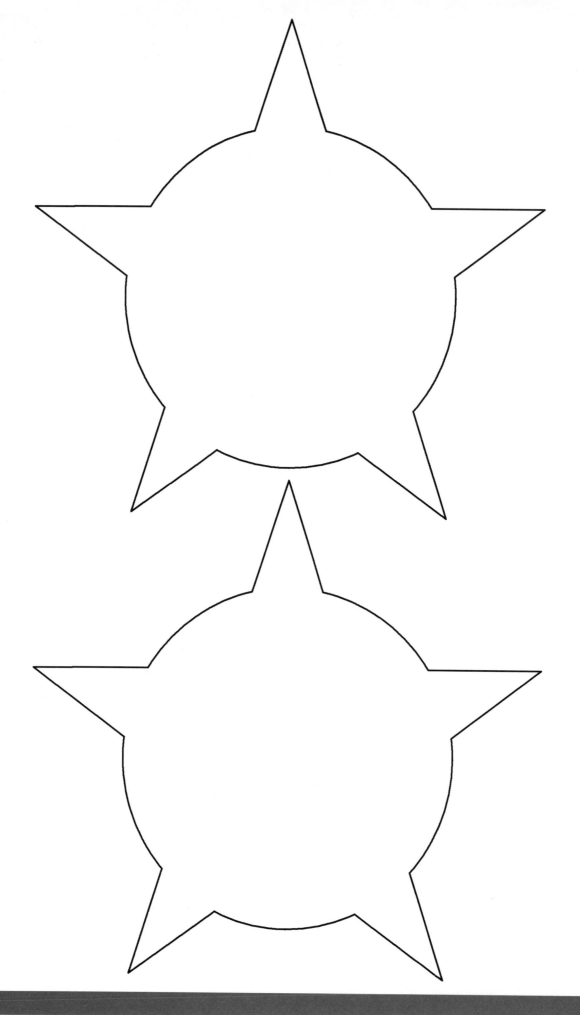

Have Courage

Enrichment Activity

Activity 3: Project—Courageous Friends & Family Members

In the three free spaces below, have your child write a short paragraph about something courageous that a friend or family member has done. Cut them out and mail them to the individuals they are about.

Cut out the paragraph strips on the other side of this page for the Project Activity.

Have Courage

Activity 4: Visual Learning

Discuss with your child the positive message below. Post the message in a visible location for your child to see it often during the month. At the end of the month, complete *Activity 5* on the other side of this sheet.

It takes courage to acknowledge mistakes and learn from them.

Have Courage

Reinforcement Activity

Activity 5: Having Courage

Record some courageous things your child has done and post in a visible location.

1. _____

2. _____

3. _____

4. _____

5. _____

Copyright© 2006 "I Care" Products & Services   (3rd Grade)

Have Courage

Reflection Activity

Activity 6: Reflection Log

Summarize your child's positive interactions during the month and reward yourself for a job well done.

Child's Name _____ **Date** _____

Name of Parent(s) _____

Record the number for each of the following questions in the box on the right.

A. How many of the workbook activities did you do with your child? ☐

B. How many positive recognitions did your child receive from teacher(s)? ☐

C. How many positive recognitions did your child receive from teachers, family members, friends, etc.? ☐

D. How many positive recognitions did your child receive from you, the parent(s)? ☐

Have Courage

D. Record five self–initiated positive activities you did with your child that were not in this month's workbook activities.

1. _____

_____

2. _____

_____

3. _____

_____

4. _____

_____

5. _____

_____

Have Patience

Message to Parents

In this age of instant gratification, it is increasingly difficult to accept what is out of our power. When children learn that it takes time to work toward their goals and plan ahead, they can adapt more easily when their wants are not immediately met.

1. COMMUNICATION

Let's Be Patient

Talk with your child about the importance of patience. What are some of the times he has to use patience at home and at school? What are some of the ways that adults have to exercise patience?

2. ROLE PLAYING

Model It

If we want our children to be patient, we have to show them patient behavior. Point out what this looks like: "I know we'd like to get right in to see the doctor, but we can be patient and wait our turn." Also point out times when it's okay to be impatient, but that the frustration can be handled appropriately. Examples: "You need to walk across the street more quickly," or "It takes grandmother longer to finish eating than it used to. Her age gives her the right to move more slowly."

Have Patience

Parenting Activities

3. TABLE TALK

Talk About It

Discuss the following with your child:

- How do you feel when you want to go out to play and I tell you that you have to wait for your little brother?
- If you're feeling impatient, what can you do?
- Do you ever make someone else wait? How do you think he feels?
- What are some times when it's important to be patient?

4. WRITING

Convincing Others

Have your child write a commercial on "Why children need patience." Also, ask him to share with you his friends' reactions to his commercial. Did they understand the message?

Have Patience

Parenting Activities

5. PHYSICAL

Settle Down

There is research on the benefits of classical music for the brain development of babies. A study by the *College Board* found that high school students who listened to classical music scored 51 points higher on verbal portions of the SAT and 39 points higher on the math portion of the SAT than students who didn't listen to any music. Establish "Quite Time" each day for 15 or 20 minutes while you listen to soft music. Even if it's just playing in the background while everyone gets ready for school or during dinner.

6. READING

Being Patient

Being patient, especially with four–year–old Willa Jean, wasn't always easy; but Ramona managed. It was how she helped her mother, who was working so that her father could go to school. Read *Ramona Quimby, Age 8*, by Beverly Cleary, with your child. Talk about some of the ways he can be more patient, and in doing so, contribute to family goals, such as saving money for a special purchase or trip. Talk about some of the ways Beverly Cleary makes Ramona seem like a real person, not just a character in a book. What makes her unique? Describe some of her inner qualities as well as her outer qualities.

Have Patience

Parenting Activities

7. COMMUNITY

Patience Then and Now

Sometimes we can better appreciate what we have when we realize what it was like for our ancestors. Using the "T-Chart" on page 129, finish the comparison of daily living which required much more patience 200 years ago than it does today.

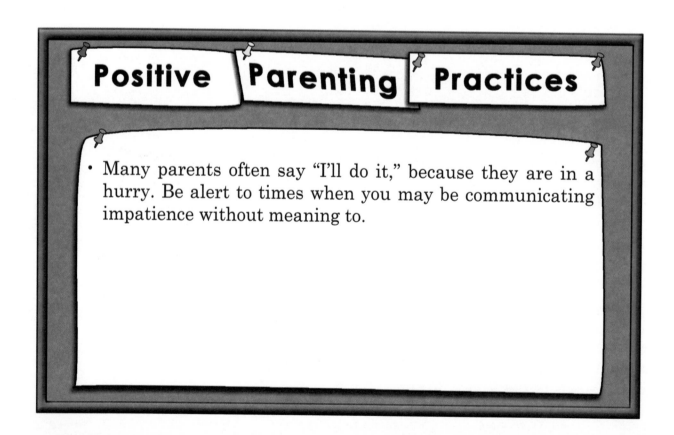

Positive Parenting Practices

- Many parents often say "I'll do it," because they are in a hurry. Be alert to times when you may be communicating impatience without meaning to.

Have Patience

Enrichment Activity

Activity 1: Community-Patience Chart

Use the "T–Chart" below for the *Community Activity* on page 128.

Then	Now
• A town crier spread the news.	
• You had to gather water from a well.	
• Every morning, the fire had to be rekindled in order to get warm.	
• Letters would take days and weeks to arrive.	
• Most food was grown or killed.	
• You had one new dress a year, if you were lucky.	
• Eating an orange was a special occasion.	
• One toy was considered enough.	
• People traveled by foot, horse, carriage, or boat.	

Have Patience

Enrichment Activity

Activity 2: Project—Get Cooking

Cooking is an activity that requires patience. Have your child help you plan and cook a special family meal. You can use favorite recipes, get a child's cookbook from the library, or go online. Follow some of the tips for safe cooking below and enjoy the results!

Tips for Safe Cooking

○ Practice makes perfect when it comes to cooking. Be patient and start slowly so you learn the techniques of chopping or slicing, always with an adult supervising.

○ Always use potholders or oven mitts, even if you think something is not hot.

○ When cooking on top of the stove, always turn your long pot handles to the side or toward the center.

○ Make sure you wash your hands well before and after handling raw meat, especially chicken.

○ Never put knives or other sharp objects in sinks filled with water. You might cut yourself when you reach into the water.

○ Keep as far away as possible from boiling water and hot oil or grease. You can get burned if the bubbles splatter.

Have Patience

Enrichment Activity

Activity 3: Project-Setting Goals

Set some goals for your child and specify the reward when the goals are achieved. Use the spaces below to document each goal and each reward. Cut them out and place them in a visible location.

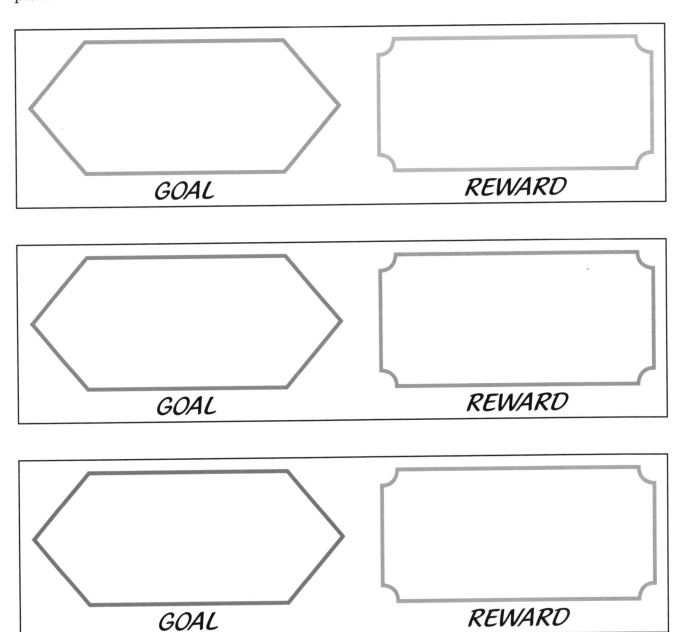

GOAL — REWARD

GOAL — REWARD

GOAL — REWARD

Have Patience

Cut out the Goals and Rewards slips on the other side of this page for the Project Activity

Have Patience

Positive Message

Activity 5: Visual Learning

Discuss with your child the positive message below. Post the message in a visible location for your child to see it often during the month. At the end of the month, complete *Activity 6* on the other side of this sheet.

Always take the time necessary to do things right.

Have Patience

Reinforcement Activity

Activity 6: Having Patience

Record times your child has demonstrated patience and post in a visible location.

1. _____

2. _____

3. _____

4. _____

5. _____

Have Patience

Reflection Activity

Activity 7: Reflection Log

Summarize your child's positive interactions during the month and reward yourself for a job well done.

Child's Name _____ **Date** _____

Name of Parent(s) _____

Record the number for each of the following questions in the box on the right.

A. How many of the workbook activities did you do with your child?

B. How many positive recognitions did your child receive from teacher(s)?

C. How many positive recognitions did your child receive from teachers, family members, friends, etc.?

D. How many positive recognitions did your child receive from you, the parent(s)?

Have Patience

D. Record five self-initiated positive activities you did with your child that were not in this month's workbook activities.

1. _____

   _____

2. _____

   _____

3. _____

   _____

4. _____

   _____

5. _____

   _____

Parenting Activities

Message to Parents

Lying is becoming more common as people strive to achieve the lifestyle they want. Take time, think through what you do and say so that they match up and send the message that truth and trust are more important than "saving face."

1. COMMUNICATION

Examples of Loyalty

Talk with your child about the importance of truthfulness and the possible consequences of lying. One lie leads to another, and pretty soon you'll get caught. You will lose respect. People won't trust you or want to be around you. Pretty soon, you'll think it's okay to do other things that are wrong.

2. ROLE PLAYING

Model It

Be aware of the little things that you say without thinking that your child could consider to be a lie. Examples could be "I'll only be on the phone a minute."; "We'll be back in a jiffy."; "The shot won't hurt."; "The cough medicine tastes like candy." Do not lie—ever! It's better to tell your child that you can't talk about something than to lie about it.

Be Truthful

Parenting Activities

3. TABLE TALK

Talk About It

Discuss the following with your child:
- Why do you think people don't like to admit it when they've done something wrong?
- If you broke your neighbor's window, why would it be a good idea to tell him?
- Do you think people who admit to making a mistake should be admired for telling the truth?
- Have you ever told a big lie? How did you feel afterward?
- Why do you think people make promises they can't keep?

4. WRITING

Honest Abe

Abraham Lincoln has often been called "Honest Abe." Challenge your child to find out why he was call this by going to a search site and typing "Honest Abe" or by going to the public library. Then, ask her to write a story about a child her age who tell the truth. Act as a scribe if her story is a long one. Maybe she'd like to illustrate it and share it with others.

Be Truthful

Parenting Activities

5. PHYSICAL

Puppet Play

They say you really learn something when you teach it to others. Help your child plan and carry out a puppet play on the importance of truthfulness. Arrange to have it given at a local day care or even a senior center. Use a children's book such as these: *The Tale of Peter Rabbit*, *The Boy Who Cried Wolf*, or *Ira Sleeps Over*. Read it several times. Then, make one puppet for each main character, following the directions on page 141. You may need to be a puppeteer along with your child, or perhaps a friend could join her.

6. READING

Tell the Truth

Telling the truth tactfully is the theme of *Honest–to–Goodness Truth* by Patricia McKissack. After reading it with your child, go over samples of how she can tell the truth without hurting someone's feelings. Examples could be when someone asks her if she likes a new hair cut and she doesn't or when she's invited to play at someone's house and doesn't want to go.

Be Truthful

Parenting Activities

7. COMMUNITY

Honesty Is the Only Policy

Keep track of the local news with your child through television or the newspaper. Look for examples of honesty. Did a politician or community leader follow through on a promise? Did a whistle blower tell the facts about a dangerous situation? Help your child write a letter thanking that person for telling the truth.

Positive Parenting Practices

- Don't put your kids in situations where lying is easier than telling the truth.

- Never ask your child to lie. Examples: "Just tell him I'm not here."; "When they ask where we've been, tell them . . ."; "Remember we can get in free if you're under . . ."; etc.

Be Truthful

Activity 1: Physical–Puppets

Use the directions and template on the next page for the *Physical Activity* on page 139.

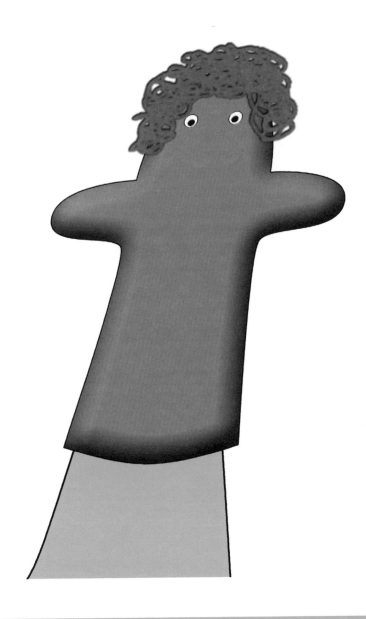

Be Truthful

Directions for Hand Puppet

1. Cut out this pattern.

2. Trace the pattern onto two pieces of felt.

3. Cut out the felt patterns.

4. Glue the felt pieces together around all edges but the bottom. You could also stitch them by machine or by hand.

5. Draw features on the front of the puppet. Permanent markers or fabric paint work well. Add googly eyes if you'd like. You can even glue yarn onto the head for hair.

6. Practice moving the puppet.

Be Truthful

Activity 2: Art—Honor Code

More and more schools have honor codes to encourage students to demonstrate. Some are simple sentences like "We strive to build a community based on respect, honesty, and courage." Others are like a "To Do" list. Work with your child to develop an honor code either for herself or for all the children in the family. You'll find some ideas on what to include below, but include what's appropriate for your family. Have your child write out the code and create a border around it. Cut it out and hang it where you can refer to it from time to time.

Pick some of the following for your honor code or write your own list.

- If you promise to do something, do it!

- If a cashier gives you extra money by mistake, return it.

- Don't have someone else do your homework.

- Tell the truth to everyone.

- Keep your eyes on your own paper.

- If you find someone else's property, return it.

- Keep secrets.

- Don't make excuses.

- Admit it when you make a mistake.

Be Truthful

Enrichment Activity

Activity 3: Project—Keeping Score

It's important for you to acknowledge all of the messages your child will get that indicate that "little lies won't hurt anyone." They are everywhere in the media. Using the score cards below, watch four of your child's favorite television shows. Make a check mark on the score card each time someone says something that is obviously not true, an exaggeration, or the truth. Which is most common? If it is lies and exaggerations over truth, maybe you should steer her to watching other shows.

Respecting the Truth

Show:

True	Not True	Exaggera-tion

Respecting the Truth

Show:

True	Not True	Exaggera-tion

Respecting the Truth

Show:

True	Not True	Exaggera-tion

Respecting the Truth

Show:

True	Not True	Exaggera-tion

Activity 4: Visual Learning

Discuss with your child the positive message below. Post the message in a visible location for your child to see it often during the month. At the end of the month, complete *Activity 5* on the other side of this sheet.

The truth will always give you lasting freedom.

Be Truthful

Reinforcement Activity

Activity 5: Being Truthful

Record when your child told the truth and post in a visible location.

1. _____

2. _____

3. _____

4. _____

5. _____

Be Truthful

Reflection Activity

Activity 6: Reflection Log

Summarize your child's positive interactions during the month and reward yourself for a job well done.

Child's Name _____ **Date** _____

Name of Parent(s) _____

Record the number for each of the following questions in the box on the right.

A. How many of the workbook activities did you do with your child? ☐

B. How many positive recognitions did your child receive from teacher(s)? ☐

C. How many positive recognitions did your child receive from teachers, family members, friends, etc.? ☐

D. How many positive recognitions did your child receive from you, the parent(s)? ☐

D. Record five self–initiated positive activities you did with your child that were not in this month's workbook activities.

1. _____

   _____

2. _____

   _____

3. _____

   _____

4. _____

   _____

5. _____

   _____

Recommended Books

To order a set of books that corresponds to the Positive Parenting Activities in this Workbook, or to order additional Workbooks from the "Unleash the Greatness in Your Child" Series or "I Care" books (see following pages), fill out the order form below. Then, cut the form along the dotted line and tear out the card along the perforation. Send the card along with check, money order, or credit card information in an envelope and mail it to the address shown on the card. You can also place your order at www.icarenow.com/parents.html, or e–mail the information requested on the card to parents6@icarenow.com.

3rd Grade Book Pack $51.95

Amber Brown Sees Red
Call It Courage
Felicity Saves the Day
Harriet Tubman: Call to Freedom
Honest–to–Goodness Truth
King Midas and the Golden Touch
Perfect Pigs: An Introduction to Manners
Ramona Quimby, Age 8
Secret Shortcut, The
Take the Court
Uncle Jed's Barbershop
Who Is a Stranger and What Should I Do?

	$51.95
Tax @ 7%	$3.64
S & H @ 10%	$5.20
Total:	**$60.79**

- -

	Quantity	Price	Total	Method of Payment:
3rd Grade Book Pack		$51.95		☐ Check
"Unleash the Greatness In Your Child" Workbook Series		$19.95		☐ Money Order
Indicate Grade Level				☐ Credit Card
"I Care" Parental Involvement—Engaging Parents to Improve Student Performance Book		$14.95		
☐ English ☐ Spanish		Subtotal		Name on Card
		Tax @ 7%		Credit Card Number
		S & H @ $5.00 or 10% (whichever is greater)		
		Grand Total		Expiration Date

Workbook Series

Unleash the Greatness in Your Child Workbook Series   **$19.95/ea.**

Workbook Grade Level — Available

Workbook Grade Level	Available
Toddler	May 2006
Pre–Kindergarten	Now
Kindergarten	Now
1st Grade	Now
2nd Grade	Now
3rd Grade	June 2006
4th Grade	June 2006
5th Grade	Now
6th Grade	July 2006
7th Grade	August 2006
8th Grade	September 2006
9th Grade	September 2006
10th Grade	October 2006
11th Grade	October 2006
12th Grade	October 2006

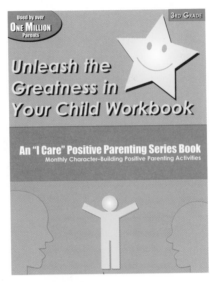

	$19.95
Tax @ 7%	$1.40
S & H @ $5.00 or 10% (whichever is greater)	$5.00
Total:	**$26.35**

Additional copies for individuals of *Unleash the Greatness in Your Child* Workbooks can be purchased at www.amazon.com, www.borders.com, www.barnesandnoble.com (or www.bn.com), and in Barnes & Noble book stores.

Schools and school systems can order additional copies at www.icarenow.com.

- -

Mail to:

_____
Name

_____
Street Address

_____
City   State   ZIP

_____
Telephone (Optional)

_____
E-mail Address (Optional)

"I Care" Parenting Manual
P.O. Box 492
906 Elmo Street
Americus, GA 31709

50 Ways Parents Can Say "I Care"

1. Post & Discuss Positive Messages
2. Attend Teacher/Parent Conferences
3. Take Family Portraits
4. Post Affirmation Pledges
5. Eat Meals Together
6. Post Daily Schedule
7. Assign Chores
8. Make Scrapbooks Together
9. Cook Meals Together
10. Award Certificates
11. Watch Movies Together
12. Visit Theme Parks
13. Volunteer at School
14. Read Books to Each Other
15. Attend Family Events
16. Give Parties for Special Occasions
17. Schedule Board Game Nights
18. Visit the Zoo
19. Help with a Class Project
20. Monitor TV Programs
21. Attend Parenting Workshops
22. Send Get Well Cards to Friends & Family
23. Lunch with Mom
24. Lunch with Dad
25. Encourage Hobbies
26. Attend Sport Events
27. Attend Local Theatre
28. Provide Enrichment Activities
29. Schedule Ice Cream Socials
30. Visit the Library
31. Go Shopping Together
32. Attend Friends' Events
33. Help with Homework
34. Post a Child Affirmation Pledge
35. Enroll Child in Book Club
36. Go Fishing Together
37. Go Skating Together
38. Encourage Creativity
39. Discuss Child's Day
40. Praise Good Efforts
41. Say *I Love You* Often
42. Write Notes to Recognize Achievement
43. Document Positive Activities
44. Talk About Positive Activities
45. Role Model Desired Behaviors
46. Support Extracurricular Activities
47. Schedule Family Nights
48. Attend Community Events
49. Help with School Projects
50. Set Limits

"I Care" Parental Involvement Book

"I Care" Parental Involvement—Engaging Parents to Improve Student Performance, by Elbert D. Solomon, is full of research–based, field–tested implementation practices and measurement tools and introduces an innovative curricular approach to parental involvement that will delight parents, teachers, and students. More importantly, it will improve student performance, help parents to initiate more positive activities with their children at home, and enable educators to get beyond the difficulties of involving parents. Available in English and Spanish.

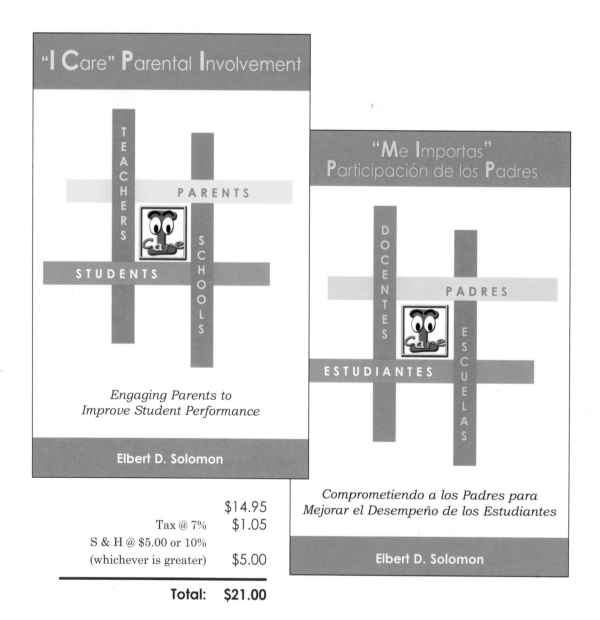

	$14.95
Tax @ 7%	$1.05
S & H @ $5.00 or 10% (whichever is greater)	$5.00
Total:	**$21.00**